BY GITA MEHTA

Karma Cola
Raj
A River Sutra
Snakes and Ladders

SNAKES AND LADDERS

GITA MEHTA

Snakes
and
Ladders

GLIMPSES OF MODERN INDIA

18212

ANCHOR BOOKS
DOUBLEDAY

NEW YORK   LONDON   TORONTO   SYDNEY   AUCKLAND

AN ANCHOR BOOK
PUBLISHED BY DOUBLEDAY
a division of Bantam Doubleday Dell Publishing Group, Inc.
1540 Broadway, New York, New York 10036

ANCHOR BOOKS, DOUBLEDAY, and the portrayal of an anchor are
trademarks of Doubleday, a division of
Bantam Doubleday Dell Publishing Group, Inc.

Snakes and Ladders was originally published in the United States
by Nan A. Talese/Doubleday in 1997. The Anchor Books edition is
published by arrangement with Nan A. Talese/Doubleday.

Page 299 represents a continuation of this copyright page.

Book design by Marysarah Quinn

The Library of Congress has cataloged the hardcover edition of this
book as follows:
Mehta, Gita.
Snakes and ladders: glimpses of modern India / Gita Mehta.
— 1st ed.
p.   cm.
1. India—Description and travel.
FS414.2.M44
954—dc21   96-49004
CIP

ISBN 0-385-49169-7

DEDICATED TO

the sole country under the sun that is endowed
with imperishable interest for alien prince and
alien peasant, for lettered and ignorant, wise
and fool, rich and poor, bond and free, the one
land *all* men desire to see, and having seen once,
by even a glimpse, would not give that glimpse
for the shows of all the rest of the globe combined.

—MARK TWAIN (1897)

CONTENTS

Foreword   xv

PART ONE

1. Freedom's Song   3
2. Who's Afraid of Being Indian?   18
3. My Damned Soil   24

PART TWO

4. Banish Poverty   45
5. Banish Charity   55

6. Reinventing the Wheel   65

7. Food for Thought   73

8. New Money   84

9. An Embarrassment of Riches   91

10. Typing   104

11. Dreaming   114

12. Writing   119

13. The Voice of the People   124

14. Management Crisis   128

PART THREE

15. Last Rites   133

16. Finding the Center   139

17. Congress Culture   144

18. Nonviolence   149

19. Good Housekeeping   157

20. Hereditary Democracy   163

21. Mass Transit   166

22. Losing It   176

23. God's Work   180

24. Stamping   191

25. The Greatest Show on Earth   193

PART FOUR

26. Getting There   211

27. Reading   214

28. Indian Decor   223

29. Filming   230

30. Communications   241

31. Trees   248

32. Love Song of India   263

33. The Old Ways   272

34. The Shape of Things   283

35. Leisure Activity   286

Political Chronology   291

Acknowledgments   299

I should be sorely tempted, if I were ten years younger, to make a journey to India—not for the purpose of discovering something new but in order to view in my way what has been discovered.

—JOHANN WOLFGANG VON GOETHE (1787)

FOREWORD

India became self-governing in 1947. Living through our first half-century of nationhood has been a roller-coaster ride, the highs so sudden we have become light-headed with exhilaration, the lows too deep to even contemplate solution, as if the game of Snakes and Ladders had been invented to illustrate our attempts to move an ancient land toward modern enlightenment without jettisoning from our past that which is valuable or unique.

The traditional Indian game of Snakes and Ladders is simple enough, played by rolling dice to determine how many squares a player may move his marker across a board, starting at square one and finishing at square one hundred. Because of its unpredictability it was one of our favorite games when we were children. There was the element of chance determined by the throw of the dice. But more than that, the actual board was suggestive of danger, an austere geometry of squares broken by angled ladders and snakes with yawning jaws. Landing at the foot of a ladder meant you could climb it, sometimes moving thirty squares in a single throw. That was the good part. You could also make it all the way to square ninety-nine, only to encounter a snake painted in lurid colors. Then you had to slide down the serpent while your gleeful opponent streaked past.

Of course, like all ancient Indian games, Snakes and Ladders was devised for a purpose other than keeping children amused on rainy afternoons, and I have seen sixteenth-century cloth depictions of the game that once hung in isolated Himalayan monasteries. Just as the Indian board game of chess was designed to teach the strategies of war, so Snakes and Ladders was played ritually as Gyanbaji, the Game of Knowledge, a meditation on humanity's progress toward liberation.

Sometimes, in our glacial progress toward liberation from the injustices that make a mockery of political freedoms, it seems we Indians have vaulted over the painful stages experienced by other countries, lifted by ladders we had no right to expect. At other times we have been swallowed by the snakes of past nightmares, finding ourselves after half a century of independence back at square one.

Perhaps historians will make sense of India's early years of freedom. I find myself able to see only fragments of a country in which worlds and times are colliding with a velocity that defies comprehension. These essays are an attempt to explain something of modern India to myself. I hope others may also see in them facets of an extraordinary world spinning through an extraordinary time.

PART ONE

1

Freedom's Song

It was three o'clock in the morning and my mother was still dancing at the Roshanara Club in Delhi when her labor pains began. She was rushed to hospital and I was born an hour later.

Holding me in her arms, my godmother demanded that I be named Joan of Arc. She was a revolutionary, you see, like many of the other young people dancing that dawn. Styling themselves freedom fighters, frequently forced to go underground for their political activities against the British Empire, when they were not in jail they spent an inordinate amount of time dancing the rumba, the tango, the foxtrot, and hoping the British departure from India was imminent.

My parents lived in New Delhi, the brand-new capital designed by Lutyens for a British Empire destined to last forever, but in barely twenty years the Empire was already looking rocky and my parents were providing sanctuary to so many Indian nationalists on the run from the police that an elite of freedom fighters across the subcontinent knew my parents' home as Absconder's Paradise.

On the morning I was born a consensus of opinion in Absconder's Paradise held that Joan of Arc lacked an Indian resonance. And so I was named Gita, or song. As in song of freedom, you understand, because it was the 1940s and it seemed freedom was finally at hand. The choice of name showed a premature optimism. Exactly three weeks later six armed constables arrived at Absconder's Paradise, manacled my father, and took him off to jail.

The handcuffs had to do with the pistols. A decade of Gandhian nonviolence had not dislodged the British from India. These ardent young nationalists, mostly still in their twenties and impatient for freedom, had acquired arms from sympathetic nationalist officers in the Indian Army against the day when they might have to die on their feet rather than live on their knees. Indeed, a few years earlier my father's first cousin, a nineteen-year-old poet who had led the raid on the British Armoury at Chittagong, died on the steps of the Armoury in a volley of bullets rather than surrender, unaware that his wounded younger brother had already been captured.

As the handcuffs were placed on my father, he instructed my mother, under guise of bidding farewell, to get rid of the arms. Otherwise, it was a certainty that Father would find himself sharing a cell with his unfortunate cousin in the dreaded penal colony of Kala Pani—the Island of Black Water—one of the distant mass of Andaman Islands where only the most dangerous prisoners were incarcerated, and where conditions were so unspeakable that half of the sixty-odd prisoners who shared my uncle's life sentence, when he was deported at the age of fourteen, ended up committing suicide in their cells.

Getting rid of the arms posed a problem for my mother. Like many girls in northern India she had been raised in purdah, tutored in the seclusion of the women's quarters by a succession of women, including a Scottish governess. My mother's traditional education ensured that she could turn out a competent watercolor of the lakes of her native Kashmir, play the odd raga on the sitar, show a familiarity with the allusions of classical Sanskrit, or recite Persian quatrains. But she lacked certain modern skills.

Early in their marriage, my father set about correcting this inadequacy. Displaying a nice sense of priority, and ignoring the considerable difference in their heights, he first taught my mother ballroom dancing. Then he taught her to play bridge. Then he put her on a bicycle, pushed it until she pedaled well enough to retain her balance, and deserted her. She cycled half-way around Delhi before she had the courage to dismount, but her one lesson made her a cyclist.

Father, who was by way of being an air ace, now decided Mother should learn how to fly an airplane, and at the moment of his incarceration she was proving a demon at the controls of a Tiger Moth. But the ability to drive an automobile—so desperately required at that critical moment—was a skill in which Mother lacked proficiency. As yet, Father had only taught her how to reverse the two-seater Sunbeam Talbot convertible out of the long drive that connected Absconder's Paradise with the outside world.

Nonetheless, as soon as Father was frog-marched away, Mother chucked the pistols and rounds of ammunition into pillowcases, got into the Sunbeam Talbot, and gamely reversed out of the gates as far down the road as she could go. Leaving the motor running, she leapt out of the car, tossed the pillowcases into a ditch beyond a darkened pavement, reversed into a U-turn, and returned home, where, uncharacteristically, there were no revolutionaries to keep an eye on two small children bawling for attention—my one-year-old elder brother and myself.

The next day Mother discovered she had decanted the pistols outside the walled compound of the Chief Inspector of Police. Fortunately, even in that moment of high melodrama, my mother, with the miserliness of the good housewife, had been careful not to use her monogrammed linen, and the connection between the arms and Absconder's Paradise was never established.

As it happens, only a few months earlier Father had been handsomely complimented, even decorated, by the Vicereine of India for the large number of British civilians he had evacuated from Burma in the teeth of the Japanese advance during World War II. Landing in impossible terrain, making sortie after sortie accompanied only by an engineer, jettisoning fuel to accommodate even more women and children on the packed aircraft, Father had generally displayed that daredevilry which is later recognized as heroism but at the time is only the natural conduct of young men larking about with life and death.

Sentimentality is an early casualty of nationalist struggles. Father saw no paradox in keeping pistols for future use against the British even as he was risking his own life to save British lives. Equally, the British saw no paradox in jailing a man as a terrorist whom they had only recently lauded as a savior.

The task of living with these ironies fell to my mother. For almost four years she followed my father from jail to jail, dragging two infants with her. Smuggling letters into jail, sometimes in the soles of my brother's shoes, although my brother, with the self-importance of small children, sometimes insisted on showing the jailers his hiding place, thus lengthening my father's prison term.

After two years Mother deposited us in a convent in the hills so that she could better concentrate on trying to curtail Father's increasingly hair-raising attempts at escape. Until that blessed moment when he broke his arm in several places and she prevailed upon a revolutionary doctor to personally set the arm—upright. For months Father was frozen in the posture of a policeman stopping traffic because Mother feared her husband's height and hell-raising temperament would make him an easy target for recapture and deportation.

Meanwhile, Father was using his jail years to improve his cooking, his chess game, and to hatch schemes for destroying the British Empire. The plot dearest to his heart required him to become a textile magnate. Apparently textile factories used the same dyes and chemicals that were required for the manufacture of currency. Father was convinced that within six months of his release he could flood the subcontinent in such a tidal wave of counterfeit currency it would drown the British Raj.

Many years later, when India had been an independent country so long it was difficult even to imagine a British Empire, I telephoned my parents from Europe to say I was expecting a child. They were enthusiastic in their congratulations and demanded that I return to India for the birth. But of the long conversation I remember only the succinct observation "Then at least we will have lived to see our first grandchild born on Indian soil."

That remark made me realize for the first time that my husband and myself had not been born citizens of a free India.

In an attempt to understand what it felt like on a day-to-day basis to be a colonized people, I asked my mother, "What is your worst memory of living under British rule?"

"My worst memory?"

"Your absolute worst."

My mother considered her answer for so long I thought she was sifting through memories almost too painful to express. My father's imprisonment; herself running from one official to another trying to gain his release; sending her children off when they were still babies to live in boarding schools; deciding which of so many humiliating experiences had been the most humiliating.

Finally she said, "When I was sixteen years old, I remember walking down the railway platform with my family's oldest retainer to board a train to Lahore. Suddenly an Englishwoman sitting in a railway carriage put her hand through the window and pulled off the old man's turban. I was horrified that she could so casually insult such a dignified old man! I stood there thinking of the filthiest abuse I knew in English. Then I shouted up at her, 'How dare you? You old hag!' "

"Did the police come for you?" I asked.

"Police? What are you talking about? This Englishwoman looked at me through the train window. She had red hair. And she said, 'My dear, one day you will be an old hag too.' That is my worst memory of the British Raj."

Since traditional Indian mothers are not given to deadpan humor, I could only take what my mother said at face value.

So I asked my father what his worst memory of the Raj had been. I expected him to tell me of his school days when an irate police sergeant, for no particular reason except perhaps the heat, had smashed a truncheon on his head, splitting his scalp in a five-inch gash. Or similar experiences, not so much for the pain inflicted as for the impotence of not being able to respond. Or at the very least, the months he had spent in solitary confinement.

Instead, Father said, "Once I was asked to fly a British colonel and his adjutant to the North-West Frontier. As I was climbing into the cockpit, he said very loudly, 'My God! I'm not going up in an airplane flown by a bloody native!' Of course, he didn't have any option. So I landed in a field about a hundred miles from Quetta, the hottest place in India during the summer. And it was damned hot in that field, without a tree for miles. The colonel was sweating and abusing natives, his face getting redder and redder in the sun while his adjutant nodded obediently."

"What did you do?"

"Got back into the cockpit, told him to find someone who wasn't a bloody native to fly him, and took off, leaving him to walk to Quetta."

Over the years I have found that no amount of wheedling can get my parents or their associates to talk about their suffering. They will speak passionately about the suffering of others.

Indeed, a whole generation of the jeunesse dorée of Bengal, scions of some of India's most powerful and distinguished families, went into hiding on the docks of Calcutta, having joined the outlawed Communist Party during the Bengal famine created by the commandeering of food supplies for the Allied forces in expectation of a Japanese attack on India. When the attack did not materialize, the food was released and found its way into the black market, where ordinary people could not afford to buy it. That winter of 1942, into the spring, while tons of food rotted away, nearly three million people starved to death, most of them on the streets of Calcutta.

Decades later these doughty old nationalists are still enraged when they speak about such injustices. Decades later they still take those injustices personally. But the injustices they themselves endured are simply brushed aside as part of the necessary price of becoming citizens of a free India rather than remaining subjects of a foreign empire. And whenever they talk about those years of nationalist struggle they only joke and tell funny stories, as if it were bliss in that dawn to be alive but to be young was very heaven.

And perhaps it was. The nationalist movement broke so many of the shibboleths that constrained conventional Indian society. Women raised as my mother had been could never have hoped to live with such ease among so many extraordinary young men and women in an atmosphere of such excitement. It wasn't just the airplanes, the pistols, the deadly games of hide-and-seek with the police, the unchaperoned socializing between men and women. Their desire for freedom propelled them out of the confines of their sheltered lives and society's notions of respectable behavior into unknown worlds where they were forced to discover their own strengths.

For instance, my godmother was from a well-known Hindu family from eastern India, but she had broken iron convention by marrying a prominent nationalist who was a Muslim from northern India. Her mentor, modern India's greatest woman leader, Sarojini Naidu—who called Mahatma Gandhi "Mickey Mouse" and who was herself described by Gandhi's biographer Robert Payne as "exuberant, earthy, irreverent, improbable . . . one of those women who make the world glad"—had already shocked Indian sensibilities by marrying beneath her own high caste. Such women were fearless, whether they were on the barricades or bearding the King Emperor in his palace or leading marches against mounted police. Later that same fearlessness would take them into the middle of the worst Hindu-Muslim riots in the most crowded Indian cities during the partition of the subcontinent into the two nations of India and Pakistan, where, unarmed and unaccompanied, they would attempt to stop the killings through sheer force of will.

It is a fearlessness I find hard to understand today. Their courage did not seem to be inspired by self-aggrandizement or ideological dogma or religious fervor—those certainties which usually fuel suicidal actions—and sometimes I wonder if they did indeed possess what Mahatma Gandhi called a kind of moral force.

Hoping to grasp the nature of their courage, I spoke to the uncle who had been sentenced to the penal colony of Kala Pani. He was an affectionate man who liked to play the piano and in his seventies still displayed a childlike curiosity about the world.

But I was in absolute awe of him. Seventeen years incarcerated in a penal colony!

"Weren't you frightened when you heard your sentence?"

"Naturally. I was only fourteen years old. I had been shot in the ankle. Tortured and interrogated for weeks before being sentenced to a lifetime of hard labor, put in chains, and loaded onto the ship sailing to Kala Pani. Still, I don't think I really understood fear until we docked and I saw four British jailers in knee socks and starched white shorts cracking their whips on the sand, shouting, 'This is where we tame the Bengal tigers!'"

Then he smiled. "I wouldn't recommend my life to everyone. But I think when you face fear every day for years, and are lucky enough to survive, you learn a little about its limits. In any case, British rule was also a form of imprisonment. There was no freedom of speech, or of the press, or of congregation. At least now we are citizens of a free nation."

I suppose on paper that is true. But in the fifty years that India has been a free nation the names of those who genuinely fought for freedom have been progressively excised from our history.

Instead, we have been bored to tears by overbearing leaders who have claimed that they are India, but even worse, that India is them. And their sons. And their sons' sons, yea even unto nausea.

The latter claim, particularly, sticks in the craw, especially when they go to extreme lengths to make the claim stick, such as the wholesale imprisonment of anyone who begs to differ. And there has been too little fearlessness in defying them.

In fact, the most interesting evolution in independent India is the change from individual fearlessness in the face of social and political injustice to craven courting of those who possess social and political power.

It is a surprise when things are otherwise. I once called on a senior bureaucrat whose office was only three doors down from the office of the then Prime Minister, Indira Gandhi, who was already quite loopy and entertained a genuine conviction that her family owned India. Naturally, her intense obsession with an imagined inheritance had given rise to an equally intense paranoia with those who might deny it, and consequently her administration was colored with many examples of tale-carrying, of ambitious courtiers reporting lies about their colleagues, and all the other spy-versus-spy paraphernalia of the would-be despot.

Wont to harangue the citizenry in public speeches with such lines as "Remember! My father gave you freedom!" Mrs. Gandhi did not take lightly to government officers with an independent turn of mind. So I was astonished to hear this senior bureaucrat expressing his exasperation with the Prime Minister in such terms as "dynastic" and "paranoid" without a hint of self-consciousness.

"Should you be talking quite so loudly about the Prime Minister in this way?" I inquired with some admiration. "After all, she does employ you."

"She doesn't bloody employ me!" he snarled. "The people of India employ me. Don't you ever forget it. This is my damned soil."

Such bad humor is enough to make you want to cling to your Indian passport for another fifty years of freedom.

At least that was the thought that crossed my mind when an immigration officer at New Delhi airport inquired how long I had been resident out of India.

At my reply, he stared in disbelief. "And you are still carrying an Indian passport, madam? May I ask why?"

It was an occasion to be blunt. But I was in a land where ladies don't swear. So I couldn't bring myself to snarl, "Because this is my damned soil. And don't you ever forget it!"

2

Who's Afraid of Being Indian?

"Why does no one want to be an Indian?" the interviewer asks me, to the surprise of the other panelists sitting around the table.

We are broadcasting a radio show in London. It is early in the morning. I am staring in a bemused fashion at the person being interviewed before me.

He has been introduced, I think, as a dentist from Birmingham. But he is dressed as an American cowboy. Ten-gallon hat, chaps, six-guns. Although it is a radio interview, he has just demonstrated how fast he can draw his six-guns.

"Isn't it interesting that everyone wants to be a cowboy?" the interviewer asks the dentist as I find myself blinking into the barrels of two pistols. "Tell me, why does no one ever want to be an Indian?"

The dentist is holstering his guns and misses the question, so the interviewer turns to me. "Well, why do *you* think no one ever wants to be an Indian?"

"I suppose," I reply as I watch the dentist warily, "some of us have it thrust upon us."

There is a burst of nervous laughter from the other panelists. They have registered the sari, the red spot on my forehead, the markings of another kind of Indian but one no less capable of taking the innocent question as some sort of racial insult. But it would have interested the immigration officer who could not understand how, having had the opportunity to become a denizen of the First World, I had not seized the chance to do so.

Such incomprehension is not unique, as any immigration official from the First World will confirm. Among the most obvious trends in current history is the movement of people from colonial countries that have only recently gained their freedom toward the very countries their forbears expended so much energy to expel. The question is why.

From my childhood I still have vivid memories of getting into slanging matches with other children about comparative nationalities. Our opponents were ruddy-complexioned, blond-haired children from the West wearing fancy blue jeans and crinoline skirts—it was the fifties—who jeered at us, a group of plain Janes in well-oiled plaits and sober clothes that covered the arms and legs.

"What have you got but snakes and monkeys?" they yelled. "Indians are just poor and dirty and backward!"

Goaded beyond endurance, we shouted back, "Well, we built the Taj Mahal!"

"Hundreds of years ago!" they sneered. "What can you do now?"

"Well," we said. "Well . . ."

Even then it was clear to us we could be respected for the richness of our past but were not given much chance of a future. After all, the grim statistics of the present were the realities of our youth, a burden of social and economic disparity that even the most Herculean endeavor seemed powerless to reverse. Whereas these self-confident dwarfs from the First World only had to worry about what they were going to buy next. Damned unfair, we muttered. Why couldn't we be one of them?

In other words, why can't we all be cowboys? Why does anybody have to be an Indian?

Because to be an Indian today is to be assaulted by the enormity of the tasks we have inherited with freedom.

There are too many of us.

Our literacy levels are too low.

Half of us live below the poverty line.

Corruption has become the standard in those who are in public service at every level. As Piloo Mody, a Member of Parliament, once pointed out to his offended colleagues, "In India it is an indignity to post a letter, get a telephone, put a child into school, seek medical help, find a job, buy a train ticket."

But I think it is astounding that India has a Parliament at all.

A sense of impotence differentiates us from the generation that fought for India's independence. "What is the point of voting?" a man on the street replied when asked how he would vote during one of India's general elections. "The government is a flop, the country is a flop, and everything is just getting flopper and flopper."

Yet we enjoy that supreme consolation of freedom—kicking the bums out. And seventy percent of the Indian electorate avails itself of such consolation at every general election.

To me, one of the miracles of this war-weary century is India's continued existence as a democracy. A concept invented in Greece two thousand years ago for a tiny city-state has been expanded in India to include nine hundred million people in a gigantic debate on the future.

One out of every six people on the planet is an Indian—engaged in creating a mutually acceptable world. Reality, no matter how unpalatable, cannot be denied in such a massive public forum. With each election comes a greater demand for accountability, a greater insistence that problems be addressed. With each increase in accountability comes an increased sense of individual power, a refusal to settle for the injustices of the past. Such effrontery has already carried half our population, many of whom once lived below the poverty line, into the light of possibility. This has been achieved in the first fifty years of our freedom.

So when I am asked today why bother to be an Indian, I cannot confess to any very noble reason. Just an avid curiosity about the future.

Can you imagine if, by democratic consensus, the other half of our population was lifted above the poverty line and we created a country in which every citizen is able to sit down at the table?

That's one sixth of the human race.

Can you imagine what that would mean for India?

Can you imagine what that would mean for the world?

3

My Damned Soil

The thing is, I am not sure what India is. Or, to paraphrase the Rig Veda, even *if* it is.

The closest I have ever come to a definition was when I was driving through a jungle in eastern India and chanced upon a wooden plaque nailed to a tree on which someone with an imperfect grip on the English language but with an enviable self-confidence had painstakingly printed WELCOME TO INDIA—LAND OF HOARY ANTIQUITE AND FABULOUS CONTRAST. And from the days of "hoary antiquite" there is a story that suggests another definition.

The way this story goes, many centuries ago two of India's greatest sages met for a sort of spiritual showdown. One sage was a great ascetic who had achieved indestructibility after spending a lifetime performing the most arduous penances. Fittingly, he was known as the Diamond-Hard Ascetic. The other was a poet who had done no penances at all, and yet was considered the holiest man in India. He was revered as the Field of Experience.

Angered that the poet was respected more highly than himself, the ascetic thrust a sword into the reluctant poet's hands, defying the poet to wound him. The poet obediently raised the sword and struck the ascetic a mighty blow. The sword shattered but made no mark on the ascetic. Then the Diamond-Hard Ascetic brought his own sword down on the poet with all his superhuman strength, hoping to cleave the Field of Experience in two. The sword passed harmlessly through the poet's body, and the mortified ascetic acknowledged the poet as his master. Penances had only gained the ascetic strength. The Field of Experience had gone beyond strength.

It is a cliché to say that India is not really a nation. Certainly it is not a nation with the diamond-hard convictions of national identity that inspire many other countries. It is not even a single civilization. Rather, it is several civilizations in separate stages of development, co-existing despite their contradictions. And yet, throughout my youth there was an annual agitation in the Indian capital when top-notch types would arrive in Delhi from all parts of the land to attend the National Integration Council and discuss—unsuccessfully—what was required to forge India into a recognizable nation.

Those were the days of independent India's youth, when people in the West would aggressively demand answers from Indians to such depressing questions as "When is India going to have a revolution?" and "Why hasn't India had a Long March?"

Both the National Integrationalists and the Western interrogators failed to realize that to achieve these dramatic upheavals a country must have a cohesive identity—and India hasn't.

The annoying absence of an identity that can be controlled has always upset those in positions of power in India. It drove the bureaucrats of the British Raj crazy as they found themselves fighting a losing battle against what they saw as the chaos of India. It drove their imperial predecessors, the satraps of the Moghul Empire, into opium addiction. And the same frustrations are clearly evident in the present rulers of India, who struggle to centralize a land that has no center but is only a field of experience.

Those who believe in the dialectics of materialism or the authority of history wander through

the ruins of glorious empires and tell us India
has learned nothing from her past. Others play
statistical roulette and tell us India has no future. Professor John Kenneth Galbraith, sent by
President Kennedy as American Ambassador to
India, came up with a catchy, even accurate,
phrase when he described India as a "functioning anarchy."

For me, this lack of homogeneity which so
threatens the assembly-line sensibilities of the
end of the twentieth century is the essence of
India's genius, her greatest strength. You may
not be able to control what you can't grasp—but
you can't destroy it either.

To take the obvious contradictions first. Most
Indians view most other Indians as foreigners,
and with considerable justification. The British
governed only two thirds of India. The other
third was made up of over five hundred independent kingdoms, so the geography, the races,
the languages, the customs of India have less in
common than their equivalents among the actually separate nations of Europe or the Americas.

I once asked a man from southern India who
was working for an Indian diplomat in London
if he felt homesick, being so far from home.

"Not really," the man replied. "I am quite
used to being abroad. Before I came to London I
was working in Delhi."

27

It was a reasonable answer. India is the sum of a million worlds enclosed by oceans on three sides, by the mighty Himalayas on the north. Within these boundaries are voluptuous eastern cultures circled by rice fields and western desert kingdoms locked in stone fortifications. Descendants of India's earliest inhabitants occupy the jungles sweeping through her heartland; three-thousand-year-old sacred cities still flourish on the banks of her immense rivers; merchant cultures still grow rich from her ancient ports.

So Delhi may be the capital of the Indian nation, but the people of India see themselves as belonging to an Indian universe defying the vagaries of history. The physical features of their capital support the logic of this view. Delhi has been the center of at least seven empires, each of whose emperors were addicts of monumental architecture, and even a casual drive through the city forces one to brood on the transience of *gloria mundi*.

Behind the huge elephant gates of a fortress known simply as the Old Fort because no one can quite remember who built it, archaeologists are excavating the ruins of what they believe to be the sacred empire of the Hindu religious epic the *Mahabharata*. Down the road is the vast sandstone showpiece built to house the Viceroy of what was once the most powerful empire on earth, the British Empire. Further on is the mighty Red Fort, which housed the Viceroy's predecessors, the Moghul Emperors, who called themselves the Shadow of God on Earth and gave audience from a Peacock Throne in gem-encrusted chambers—the same fortress from whose battlements the flag of an independent nation was first unfurled when a truncated India finally kept, in the words of India's first Prime Minister, her "tryst with destiny."

That destiny was political freedom, an assurance of birthright. Only this defines the contemporary Indian.

Other definitions fall before the evidence. We are not of a single racial origin. The Aryans of the northern plains are distinct from the Dravidians of the South, and both have little in common with the Mongol inhabitants of the East. Not even language.

The government of India officially recognizes seventeen major Indian languages in which state business may be conducted. Each of these languages possesses not only its own ancient and contemporary literatures, its own newspapers, radio and television programs, and films, but also its individual script. Then we have the classical language of Sanskrit. On top of that we have over four hundred other languages, some written, others oral. And of course, as the joint language of administration we have English, a language that Indians have made uniquely their own in more than two centuries of usage.

If speaking in tongues is a mark of divine inspiration, then surely India can claim to be the most divinely inspired place on the planet. Yet linguistic politics is a sword held to India's throat, and every time some foolish chauvinist demands the imposition of one of India's many languages as the national language, the nation erupts in riots. Such passion in my view is just as it should be. To impose a common national language, with its implications of a common culture, on a country as richly diverse as India would tragically diminish us.

And of all the elements that have contributed to our diversity, nothing has so enriched the "land of fabulous contrast" as religion. Hindu, Christian, Muslim, Jain, Parsi, Jew, Buddhist, Sikh—in India there is really no escape from religion. Every river, every lake, every mountain, is the repository of some tale of divine mythology; every jungle is marked with flowers and a smear of vermilion where India's tribals have worshipped nature.

Hinduism is the religion practiced by the majority of Indians, although "majority" ceases to have a conventional meaning when one notes that over a hundred million Indians are Muslims, giving us the third-largest Muslim population of any nation on earth. Our two-thousand-year-old Christian community claims that the first Christian missionary to reach India's shores was Doubting Thomas, Christ's disciple, and that the Church in India began with him.

We have the tree under which the Buddha reached enlightenment, Hindu temples built under the guidance of the gods, mosques so vast that seventy thousand faithful can kneel together on their prayer mats for namaz. The stupas and monasteries of the Buddhist faith are carved into our mountains. The stone colossi of the Jain religion dominate our hillsides. The Parsis have their Towers of Silence and Fire Temples, which may be entered only by the followers of Zoroaster; the Sikhs, their marble-and-gold Gurudwaras. There are the cathedrals of the Roman Catholics, the Orthodox churches of the Armenians who fled the pogroms of the Ottoman Empire, the synagogues of the Jews. And there are the countless shrines that commemorate the countless holy men of India.

My favorite shrine admirably illustrates the poet W. H. Auden's definition of civilization as "the degree to which diversity is attained, unity retained." In Bombay there is a tree in the middle of a traffic island, gallantly defying the urban nightmare, housing three separate faiths while the anarchy of Bombay's traffic hurtles oblivious around it. On one side of the tree is a white plaster Christian cross. On another is a small image of the elephant-headed Ganesh, the Hindu god of protection. On the third side is a small concrete altar on which worshippers place the Koran when they pray to Allah.

At our best in India, we still have a civilized tolerance that can accommodate three faiths in one tree trunk because at its best the culture of India is like a massive sponge, absorbing everything while purists shake their heads in despair. Other cultures have sought to expel all foreign-devil influences from their shores, but India has always shown an appetite for foreign devils matched only by her capacity to make them go native.

It is as though we are unable to conceive of a culture strong enough to destroy us. Unlike those of China or Japan, the gates of India have never been closed and perhaps this has given us a special stamina. Japan was the secret kingdom, the impenetrable civilization—but where have all the kimonos gone? In India we are still wearing our saris and our dhotis not in defiant chauvinism but because quite simply that is how we dress, in spite of the fact that as late as the 1930s, when it was evident that the imperialist jig was up, an Indian official of the British Empire could still be fired if he turned up at his government office wearing native clothes.

So when I see painted on the walls of six-teenth-century Rajput villas pictures of the god Krishna playing his flute not to a herd of cows in a meadow but from the backseat of a Rolls-Royce, I feel reassured that Indian culture is still in business, that Krishna will continue to play his flute whether he is in a field, a Rolls, or a rocket.

Then again, as the rest of the world races headlong toward the bionic, sometimes I wonder if we will also be tempted by the siren songs of Disneyland and settle for a safe homogeneity. To describe one of those moments of doubt, twenty-five years ago I stumbled upon what I then per-ceived as the end of Indian culture.

I was visiting the pillared edifice in Delhi that housed the state-controlled All India Radio, the major patron of Indian culture after the court patronage of India's artists had ended. Lost in a warren of recording studios, I entered a small soundproof cell in which I found a young woman sitting behind a steel desk. Her hair was covered with an embroidered veil. In the center of her forehead was an enameled ornament held in place by a line of pearls; just visible under the silk folds covering her head were long earrings that swayed in and out of her hair as she sang.

The manner of her dress and singing indicated she was a *mushaira* girl, trained in the arts of singing and poetry from childhood, expected to hold cynical aesthetes in thrall by her ability to convert their remarks into poetic quatrains sung to melodic variations, without ever repeating herself.

The essence of her training would have been mastery of an audience, the catalyst of her artistry a dialogue with that audience. But the times had changed, and here she was in all her finery, sitting on a wooden chair instead of leaning against cushions on a richly woven carpet, seducing a microphone dangling from the perforated soundproof tiles on the ceiling, her kohl-lined eyes frantically seeking a response from the recording engineer in his glass box, who was studying his dials, not her, as she plaintively sang,

> *"The world speaks of permanence,*
> *But when I walked to the cremation*
> *ground,*
> *My path was crossed by a bridegroom."*

Had she been performing her melancholy lament in front of a live audience, she would have been showered with money and compliments. As it was, she just seemed camp. An art that had to do with dialogue had been reduced to the poutings of narcissism.

Even something as inconsequential as a *mushaira* girl singing divertissements in an isolated soundproof room is antithetical to Indian culture because of our conviction that art is not just something displayed by the talented to a passive audience, but that moment when the artist, the audience, the subject, the discipline—all combine to become something approaching religious experience, a moment of mutual creation.

One of India's great sitar maestros has described how he was trained to lead an audience to such perception when he was learning to play the Bhairava, a morning raga performed to herald the dawn. The Bhairava is a musical meditation on the transition from darkness to light, celebrating the rebirth of the day as a rebirth of the spirit. But in itself the raga is only a scale, so a musician's excellence is assessed by what he can do with that scale through improvisations which last more than an hour.

The sitar player's account of how he was taught as a young boy to play this handful of notes is an illustration of how the Indian artist learns his art. He and his fellow students would rise at three-thirty in the morning. By four-thirty they would be expected to be at their places in the courtyard of the guru's house, where the master would be waiting, a bronze oil lamp by his side. The pupils would sit before him on white sheets spread on the flagstones, sitars balanced on their left shoulders, eager to prove themselves prodigies. The guru would ask them one by one to play the first note of the raga. Believing this to be some sort of warming-up exercise, the students happily complied. Then the guru would make them play the same note again. For three hours every morning he would allow his pupils to play that single note only, teaching them to contain the aspirations of an entire raga in a single sound.

Each month the guru allowed the students to add another note to their repertoire, until they understood that they were not learning music but how to meditate. It was eight months before they were allowed to play the entire scale, two years before the guru permitted his most gifted pupil to perform the raga.

In his account of that first performance the sitar masetro records how those punishing hours of stilling his own mind, of being forced to listen to each note as if it were the primal sound, of having to concentrate on the transition from dark to light—through the different seasons—

for two whole years, gave him an understanding beyond himself or his talents, which he could reveal through music to the listener, a religious awareness he could share with his audience.

The same purpose moved those who carved the stone sculptures, built the great erotic temples, or cast the bronzes in India's cultural past. The measure of their excellence is the fact that centuries later their art is still venerated in worship, not isolated by mere admiration.

Today the government no longer wields the total control it exercised for forty long years over Indian radio and television. So, in a sense, artistic freedom has increased. But in our changing world, new media require stars instead of artists, new audiences prefer sensation to meditation. The dialogue of live performance is giving way to the monologue on record, radio, TV. Can Indian culture really withstand the twin challenges of electronic communications and marketing when young Indians are dancing to hybrid music forms like Indi-pop and Bhangra-rock; when peasant farmers possess cellular telephones; when satellites are proliferating over our skies?

It is devoutly to be hoped that we rise to the challenge and continue to have a life outside the limited world of recording studios and museums. If not, we are in trouble. Preservation is not our game. As for decay, we are hardly conscious it exists.

And yet there is a fecundity in Indian decay that suggests the possibility of coming attractions. We smell more of the compost heap than of the graveyard, showing endless ingenuity in making progress accommodate the human form.

An anthropologist once described to me a mass engagement ceremony he had attended in a desert area of western India. Fifty girls from one nomadic tribe were being engaged to fifty boys from another tribe, the idea being that when the children reached maturity they would not have to race around the desert looking for suitable mates, since they would now be assured of a future domestic life.

That night, in deference to the festivity of the occasion, the parents wore the traditional jewelry which the anthropologist had come to record—globes of beaten silver fastened to the hair with thick, intricately carved silver chains. But their children wanted higher wattage. Impatient with their fathers' silver chains and globes, the sons wore lightbulbs on their heads, strings of electrical Christmas decorations powered by batteries attached to their belts. The girls were thrilled as the desert glowed with colored lights. And the ethnic expert from the big city realized how patronizing his own attitude was. Until that night he had thought of these nomads not as people but as hangers for tribal artifacts.

In India we are still forced to remember that people are individuals as well as anthropological or economic statistics. The world has lived so long under the yoke of Malthusian projections that Indian humanity has become a dirty word, meaning only population explosions, though nothing has proved so damaging to modern India as the patronization of master-race economics, with its real fear of the poor and therefore its unsaid but unmistakable view of them as subhumans who must be forced to accommodate to the logic of economics.

The fact is that even if half of us dropped dead and the population ceased populating entirely, we could not become some sanitized suburbia, never turn into Singapore. We are a continent, not a city—a continent that, despite its own inertia, the unwieldiness of its massive bureaucracy, the venality of its leaders, the centuries-old institutionalized injustices of its social systems, has consistently proved the prophets of doom more wrong than right.

We were told we could never survive as a democracy, because a hungry man can have no understanding of freedom. I even heard the British humanitarian Malcolm Muggeridge say on a

British television program, "People whose stomachs are empty have no idea what democracy means." Fortunately, a former British Foreign Minister was also on the program and spoke for India when he succinctly observed that such views "make me want to throw up."

And if statistics have any magic, here are some to counter the prophecies of the pessimists. India is among the ten most industrialized nations on earth. We turn out five million university graduates a year. We have a space program in advance of many Western European countries. Most important, we are self-sufficient in food.

The reverse side to these statistics is that self-sufficiency in food has not been matched by efficiency in getting food to the mouths of the hungry. The huge increase in university graduates has not been equaled by the production of jobs to absorb them. The ability to launch satellites into space does not disguise the lack of irrigation and electrification on the ground.

Even a casual visitor cannot fail to observe that the diversities of India's past are more than matched by the immense complexities of her present, her problems infinitely more complicated than the simplistic solutions offered either by her own leaders or by experts from abroad. Indeed, Mahatma Gandhi, whom many Indians call the father of the nation, once said any solution to India's problems could at best be valid for about ten years. Well, we've survived five times that number of years as an independent country and we still retain the privileges of freedom—a secret ballot, a free press, an independent judiciary.

We haven't set fire to the past on the specious grounds that only the destruction of the past would allow us a future. We haven't indulged in wholesale institutional savagery on the equally specious grounds that only cruelty to present generations will ensure Utopia for future ones.

And yet India progresses, a monumental juggernaut of contradictory realities.

Have we been lucky? Or, even, great? Who knows?

Indians don't. They only shrug and say, "That is Bharat. That is India."

PART TWO

4

Banish Poverty

"You must have seen the people foraging through that huge garbage dump on the outskirts of Delhi," the Indian paper tycoon remarked.

"The beggars, looking for food?" I asked. "Of course I've seen them."

But that was all I had done. Seen them, then quickly turned away, covering my nose although the car windows were rolled up and the banks of the four-lane highway were planted with bougainvillea bushes to hide a square mile of fetid garbage with vultures circling overhead.

"They're not beggars," the tycoon corrected me. "They are ragpickers—supplying raw material to us in the paper industry."

I was shocked. "You mean people working in

those subhuman conditions are on your payroll?
You hire them to live like that?"

"Of course I don't bloody hire them," he said
in irritation. "They collect rags and sell them to
a contractor. If you are looking for a convenient
phrase, you might say these people are self-employed."

Well, talk about the unacceptable origins of
capitalism.

"Actually, it's only an extension of the kind
of work they have always done," the tycoon explained kindly. "They're all untouchables by
caste. Local sweepers."

Intrigued by these self-employed people, so
evidently masters of their own destiny, I got out
of the car and made my way toward the tiny
figures in the middle of that gray landscape. The
handkerchief covering my face did little to protect me from the quicksand under my feet. Why
hadn't I realized this garbage dump would not
be solid ground? That I would be sinking into
the effluvia from the deaths, marriages, examination papers, hospital refuse of a giant metrop-
olis of nine million people?

Beyond the dump flowed the holy Jumna
River. On the far bank I could see the stone battlements of the Red Fort, where languid Moghul
Emperors had once enjoyed the evening breeze
in their marbled wind pavilions while their sub-

jects promenaded on the riverbank below. One Emperor had even famously sighed, "If there is a paradise on earth, it is this, it is this."

Today, to the left of the battlements a power station belched gray smoke into the air, coloring the mile of garbage a uniform gray, like filthy flannel. Sunk to my knees in spongy refuse, not daring to look down to see what might be clinging to my legs, I plowed my way toward a thin woman wearing a short peasant skirt and a torn jacket. She looked middle-aged but could as easily have been in her twenties. In one hand she carried a long iron spike, hooked at the bottom, which she plunged into the waste. Farther on, I could see other scavengers fishing up bits of rusty iron or stained rags. Children, their heads barely clearing the surface of the garbage, worked beside their parents.

The exhausted woman examined me suspiciously when I greeted her. Was I a government inspector about to challenge her right to be here? Or a do-gooder who would take away her children, contributing their pittance to the family's survival? The fact that I was only a voyeur seemed to reassure her and she leaned wearily on her spike to talk.

Where was she from?

Rajputana. She used the old name for the Land of Kings.

Had she always done this kind of work?

Of course not. She had only come to the city after seven consecutive years of drought had forced her husband to sell their land to a moneylender. She was a Bhoomiya.

I looked at her in surprise. The Bhoomiya people were pathfinders. Traditionally they had guided travelers through the deserts and jungles of Rajputana—knowing every water source, every edible plant, every religious sanctuary. They were paid in arable land that their families cultivated while they delivered wayfarers safely to the next stop on their journey—until trains, buses, telephones had made the work of guides irrelevant.

The other ragpickers were circling us warily. My presence had made them curious. Now they joined our conversation. A small boy was pushed forward by his mother.

He is a Bhat, the scavengers told me, one of the community of bards who once held mythic power over kings. Only Bhats had the right to recite the genealogies of royalty, or to convert great feats of battle and honor into the epic poems that were then recited throughout the countryside.

"Once our recitations commenced a royal coronation," the woman said, gently cuffing the child on the side of the head. "Now look at my child's fate. We teach him the historical poems. Otherwise they will be forgotten. And he shouts them aloud to frighten the vultures away while he looks for rags."

I thought of the tycoon's casual observation that these people were local sweepers who had chosen to become scavengers, but I was standing there in the quicksands of the Indian capital's refuse listening to tales of displacement from all over the country.

Here was a woman from a riverside fishing village in eastern India. During heavy monsoon rains the swollen river had burst its banks and submerged her village. By breaking stones for roads, she and her husband had worked their way across India until they reached the capital—a thousand miles from the lush delta of their native land.

Two girls told me they were tribals from central India. The dense jungles that had once supported their community had been destroyed first by lumber merchants, then by stone quarrying, and they had been sold by their parents to a man looking for cheap labor to work on one of the city's construction sites. When the building was complete, he had left them to survive on their own and they didn't know where to find their parents, now working in some unknown part of India as bonded labor.

Next to them a girl from southern India shyly explained that her father had been a craftsman. But three bad monsoons in a row meant the villagers could no longer afford to buy his wooden carvings. To feed his family, her father had been reduced to selling his tools, one by one, until he had none left. The family had begged for work from one village to another. They had stopped here, and her father worked as a stone mason now.

"Can't you see there are no men here?" the women asked. "While we sift through other people's filth, our men are all breaking stones for the new highway. That's what the last five years have done to us."

"What happened five years ago?"

"Haven't you heard of the Remove Poverty program?"

Of course I had, like every other Indian during Mrs. Indira Gandhi's time as Prime Minister.

Throughout the seventies the message REMOVE POVERTY had been blazoned across the country on huge banners, on billboards and posters and graffiti smeared across walls. How could anyone have ignored it? But how had that brought them here?

"The politicians said they would remove poverty and give us jobs, so we voted for them. But when we got here they didn't want to meet us. We managed to feed ourselves by working on building sites. Carrying bricks. Mixing concrete. We lived in huts made from things that other people had thrown away. Then the country's bosses decided Delhi must look beautiful. From 'Remove Poverty' their slogans changed to 'Remove the Poor.'"

They laughed at each other. "The poor are not beautiful, as you can see. While we were at work, the bulldozers flattened our huts with all our possessions inside them. We were put in buses and taken thirty miles out of town, where there is no work. No water. No food. Nothing to protect our children from the weather. Now we have fallen to this. But we fill our stomachs somehow. Thanks to him."

"Who?"

They pointed across the four-lane highway. "The Contractor."

Behind a high bank of purple bougainvillea bushes was a shanty—two pieces of canvas stretched on poles to provide a little shade for a bed made from a discarded wooden door and covered with a threadbare cotton quilt. I made my way past piles of garbage and the tall bulrushes that lent them an almost elegant air. The pastoral element was increased by the mewling of puppies nestled for warmth in a bundle of rags. As I came closer, the refuse took on a visible identity—plastic in one heap. Rags in another. Broken glass in a third. A fourth contained twisted shapes of rusting and bent iron.

A transistor radio was blaring popular film music over the traffic noise as the Contractor invited me in. He was an alert-looking runaway from a bonded labor camp in Bihar on whom fortune had smiled. A quarter of a million other bonded laborers working without wages to clear their debts were not so lucky.

But the Contractor had somehow managed to flee the moneylender demanding repayment of a loan taken out by his grandfather, which his father and himself had repaid many times over in rapacious interest rates that placed the original debt beyond hope of clearance.

He even had his own house now—number 357 in a resettlement colony. It was actually only a mud hut, but he called it his "flat" and with equal pride he referred to this shanty as his "office."

"I know I deal in filth," he said ruefully. "But filth is my Laxmi. My goddess of wealth. If I don't stay here, the ragpickers can't bring me their goods. They already spend one third of their daily earning just to take the bus to get here. That's what the government's great Remove Poverty program achieved. I give the poor wretches credit. But I have too many debtors.

Many of them will never be able to repay me. Then I will be forced into picking rags again."

In spite of the fact that he was now a money-lender, the specter of returning to the garbage dumps haunted the Contractor. His office was an illegal construction. Government bulldozers could appear on the horizon at any moment.

Beyond the discards from an urban world stretched fields of young wheat, the green of manicured lawns. I could see veiled women in brightly colored long skirts with brass pots balanced on their heads walking toward a well. Picturesque peasants in turbans tended their oxen or piled hay into high wooden carts. This serene rural landscape was the sleight of hand by which India could make even poverty acceptable. But the truth was, a few bad breaks and the picturesque peasants could join the faceless transients across the highway trying to make a living from the steaming gray garbage dump.

And how many stories of wasted human lives were there in this place? I asked a medical officer who worked among the slum dwellers. At first he tried to give me the government line. The ragpickers were making a valuable contribution to the recycling industry. When I pressed him, he finally admitted, "We have no means of counting the number of people who are working as ragpickers even in Delhi, let alone the rest of the country. Are there hundreds of them? Thousands? No one really knows. Actually, no one has tried to find out. They are a floating and faceless group of people. But at least give them this. They do something. They do not beg."

A sanitation official in the Delhi Municipal Corporation was more honest. "We great Indians! It has become second nature in us to tolerate what is beneath human dignity in others, just so long as we ourselves remain untouched by it. These people would not be collecting and selling dirt if the government could create other jobs for them. But the government is happy spending fortunes to make sure only slogans are heard by every Indian."

Then he added bitterly, "Imagine if all that money was spent on giving them decent work."

5

Banish Charity

"When do you next get paid?" a friend asked me one evening, adding severely, "Make sure you give the money to me."

I stared pointedly at her jewelry. "And why should I do that?"

"We are trying to buy some women out of bonded labor."

I wasn't as surprised as I should have been by her bluntness. I knew she had worked in the industrial city of Ahmedabad with women who earned their living in circumstances no better than the garbage dumps of the nation's capital a thousand miles away.

Except for one thing. These women owned their own bank.

In the early fifties, years before feminism became a catchword in the West, the poorest women in Ahmedabad had pooled the meager sums they earned by scavenging in refuse dumps, pulling handcarts, selling rags, breaking stones for roads, carrying bricks in cane baskets on their heads, and they had started their own cooperative bank. They called themselves SEWA, the Self Employed Women's Association.

Their bank enabled them to take out loans and invest in such things as a sewing machine for making garments to sell. As soon as one group's initial investment was returned, another group took out another loan to start another cottage industry and become economically secure. Some members borrowed money to join training facilities and gain skills that would later allow them to form their own small commercial units. Others continued to ply their usual trades. But the women were no longer hostage to moneylenders eager to turn their despair into limitless profit. Their own bank stood between them and such exploitation.

It was no accident that SEWA should have started in Ahmedabad, the capital of India's western state of Gujarat, where the trading energy of Britain's East India Company combined with the commercial skill of Ahmedabad's prudent merchants to make the city a center not just of the textile trade but also of union activity. By the turn of the century workers in its many textile mills had formed the Textile Labour Association, one of India's oldest and best organized labor unions, blessed by Mahatma Gandhi, whose ashram was on the outskirts of the city. Perhaps Gandhi's proximity moved the daughter of a rich man to unionize the workers in her father's textile factories, where conditions were so terrible that workers were happy to spend their entire week's wages getting drunk on country liquor sold from stills conveniently set up outside the factory gates on payday. When they got home, they soundly beat their wives for asking for money to buy food for the children.

But the wives couldn't feed their children by working in the city's many factories. Women employed in the organized sectors of Indian industry were rare. Even today less than four percent of unionized labor are women, their numbers shrinking every year as men force them from protected workplaces in the intense competition for limited jobs, which are the dream of millions of "casual labourers" scratching a living on the very edge of survival. Most women, and often their children, belong to the huge population of unorganized labor, made homeless by drought and debt, vulnerable to any exploitation in its migration from the countryside to the city in search of work.

This vast shifting sea of poverty has become the focus of increasing numbers of voluntary organizations, often led by women. In Ahmedabad the desperate wives, only one step away from prostitution in the struggle to feed their families, were urged by a young middle-class woman, Elaben Bhatt, to form a union. The Self Employed Women's Association was founded in 1952. Today SEWA's bank in Ahmedabad boasts twenty-five thousand savings accounts, owned by its thirty thousand members.

The acronym SEWA means "service" in Hindi, and branches of the union can now be found all over India. In the North it has enabled sequestered women from the most orthodox Muslim families to set up embroidering units and earn enough to educate their children and still set aside money for the day they might peremptorily be divorced by their husbands with the verbal dismissal "Talak." In the South it has helped low-caste Hindu women to break the chains of illiteracy and start small businesses to market their crafts. From the hill communities of the East to the desert communities of the West, units of SEWA have encouraged self-employment and economic independence. Its members have created their own crèches and schools and medical dispensaries, taught each other hygiene and midwifery and nursing. Now the association is held up to the world as an example of self-help, to be imitated by poor nations everywhere. And it has led to numerous imitations in India itself.

One such imitation was formed in Delhi by six women working in different areas of craft development. Enraged that the unique skills and art forms that are the glory of India's handicrafts had been reduced over the years to unusable bric-a-brac sold on city pavements by ignorant middlemen eager to exploit the tourist and "ethnic" markets, they decided to combine their experience to help craftsmen. Though themselves from privileged backgrounds, the women called their organization Dastkar—one who works with his hands—and their goal was the continued employment of craftsmen who were losing their livelihoods to factory-made products.

Dastkar was aware that every sector of Indian society—from its jungle communities to its most cosmopolitan cities—has its own tradition of craft. They knew that craft is still India's second-largest employer after agriculture, with a whole government department to look after its interests—the Handlooms and Handicrafts

Board of India. After all, before mechanization, all goods had been manufactured by hand, and even now India's thousands of differing worlds produce a huge span of distinctive handicrafts, often using highly sophisticated processes and affording vast numbers of women a livelihood. But today, the laboriously handmade products must compete with mass production and sophisticated marketing techniques to attract not just city dwellers but also villagers dazzled by the advertisements they see every day on their television screens.

Convinced that no amount of government protection could make people buy what they didn't want, Dastkar asked itself how it could help craftsmen to survive in the new marketplace. Commercial and marketing expertise was the obvious answer. And it was not something village artisans possessed.

By working intensively with groups of artisans to produce crafts adapted to modern usage; by teaching them accounting, bookkeeping, and how to acquire competitively priced raw materials; by taking artisans who have never ventured outside their villages into the cities to see for themselves what the consumer wants to buy, Dastkar is trying to develop modern markets that can be sustained.

One of the original founders was the friend who was now demanding my money.

"Who are these women you are trying to help, anyway?" I asked, putting up a fight to keep the money I needed for a trip to the South.

"Tribal women and their kids. They are working as bonded labor in a silk-weaving center, practically chained to their looms."

My trip to the South evaporated in fumes of momentary guilt. "It's not very much," I said apologetically as I began signing traveler's checks.

She palmed my money, observing acidly, "Dollars go a long way in India."

A few weeks later I returned to Europe, and heard nothing further from her.

It was eighteen months before I saw my friend again, at a rather grand dinner party in the Indian capital.

Dodging ambassadors and businessmen busily discussing the opening up of the Indian economy and whether the unleashing of market forces could make India into another Asian Tiger, I caught up with her at the buffet table.

"Oh, I've been meaning to write to you," she said in an offhand way. "But I've been busy."

I was rather hurt. I felt she could at least have acknowledged my gift as being helpful. I didn't know that her organization was into self-reliance, not gratitude. Or that they ran forty units all over the country with a total capital base of only fifteen thousand dollars.

Noticing my dismay, she relented. "The money bought about one hundred and sixty women and their families out of bondage."

I was stunned. I had given her only a few hundred dollars. "One hundred and sixty women?"

"How big do you think the original debts were, for goodness' sake?" she asked, irritated. "Two hundred or three hundred rupees, that's all."

Now I knew the price of human life in India. Indeed, one stark analysis of bonded labor by the Indian School of Social Sciences showed just how much you could get for your money. In a single northern village farmer Minu had borrowed Rs. 500 ($14) to buy food and was still working off the interest on his debt after seventeen years. Farmer Nanda had borrowed Rs.100 ($3) for food and already had labored without wages for twelve years. Farmer Sukha had worked ten years to pay off a loan of Rs. 20 (75 cents) to buy a wooden box.

"What are the women doing now?" I asked my friend as she examined the dishes on the buffet table.

"They were determined to compete with their previous owners, so we loaned them money to buy their own looms and weave their own silk."

To imagine such courage, you have to imagine the cruelty of their owners, men capable of buying other human beings and feeding them just enough so that they and their children can keep on working, while their husbands are used as beasts of burden elsewhere.

She speared a leg of chicken and put it onto her plate. "In fact, I've just come back from Bombay, where we have had an exhibition of their work."

"Did you manage to sell it?" I asked with proprietary concern.

"Oh, it wasn't for sale, just display for future orders. They haven't got anything left to sell. Everything the women produce is of such high quality the exporters grab it."

She chewed at the chicken leg, oblivious to the impact her story was having. "In fact, the men who used them as slave labor are now offering to buy their output at twice the price the exporters pay because the quality is so good."

"Are they making money?"

She nodded, her mouth full.

"Well, what do they do with their money?" I persisted.

She wiped her lips. "Send their kids to private schools. They think if you pay for education instead of going to a government school, your kids will get a better education."

"Can I give them some more money?"

She was annoyed. "Certainly not. They don't accept charity. Six months ago they paid back every penny of your money. Now they are giving us money, to loan to other women. Nearly as much as you did."

Two gentlemen, complaining about India's economy, forced their way between us to reach the table.

"We are caught in a vicious cycle of poverty," one stated as he reached for a plate.

"Our tax base will never be large enough to support our population," the other agreed. "There's nothing we can do about it."

My friend had already turned away or she could have told them they were wrong. After all, she had just finished telling me how one hundred and sixty enslaved women had gone from bondage to philanthropy—or was it banking?—in a single year. And unlike us, they didn't even know the meaning of the words.

6

Reinventing the Wheel

The spinning wheel, long the center of the Indian flag, acknowledges that textiles are a living Indian art form still producing masterpieces equal to those of the past. But it also highlights the great debate in India about the traditional worker's function in our future.

Two tales from Indian mythology illustrate what the weaver means to India. The first story is about the Mother Goddess of the subcontinent, who one day took the form of a cosmic spider and began spinning a web of cotton thread. The web grew until it covered India, and still the goddess spun. Finally her immense web reached beyond the boundaries of the Himalayan mountains to enmesh the god of the Aryans—a god of progress and mechanical skills—binding him to India.

The myth of the spider goddess and the Aryan god of machines is an uncanny foretelling of the European connection with India. Europe may have come East looking for spices, but within decades Europe was inextricably bound in the web of India's textiles. Bandana, chintz, muslin, calico—all were Indian words and techniques. From the rich hangings woven with threads of gold and silver which adorned the homes of European aristocrats to the bandanas worn by the slaves working the cotton and sugar plantations of the Americas, from the fine muslins which provided the Barbary sashes of the gentlemen of North Africa and the turbans of the nobles of the Turkish Levant to the chintz furnishings favored by English ladies who dressed in calico lawn, it was the magic worked by the hands of the Indian weaver which created fortunes of such enormity that the nations of Europe fought for supremacy over India's cloth.

When Britain won the last battle for supremacy, the wealth flowing from the trade in Indian textiles turned a British trading company into the greatest empire on earth—which in its turn imported those gods of progress, the machines of the industrial revolution, into India.

The second myth is from the Indian epic the

Mahabharata. A beautiful and virtuous queen is lost by her husband in a gambling game to an evil king. The captive queen is brought into the king's audience chamber, where he is sitting upon his throne surrounded by nobles and soldiers. The king demands his prisoner be stripped naked before the lustful eyes of the assembly. The laughing guards grab the queen's garments and begin to pull. Weeping for her modesty, she begs the gods to protect her honor, and lo, even as the guards pull at her clothes, the fabric multiplies. The guards continue pulling, but there is no end to the queen's garment. Billowing cloth covers the pillars and arches of the audience chamber until it reaches the dome above the king's head.

Prisoner queens may belong to ancient mythologies, but it was in the harsh political realities of this century that Indian nationalists again used cloth to defend India's honor, calling it "the livery of our freedom." Raw cotton exported to the mills of Manchester and Lancaster was robbing Indian weavers of the source of their income, so homespun cloth woven in defiance of the power looms of the British Empire became the uniform of the Indian nationalist. Later it would become a symbol of self-reliance for free India.

Ironically, the earliest factories Indians were

permitted to own by their British masters were textile mills. In the century that followed, capital and technology generated from those early textile mills led to such wide-scale industrial expansion that India is now numbered among the ten most industrialized nations on earth.

This precise paradox—craft or machine, an ancient culture or contemporary progress—haunts India today. A large school of Indian thought believes the spinning wheel as the center of the Indian flag is emblematic of everything backward in India. Symbols once useful in expelling a foreign empire and its exploitations are now dangerous anachronisms in a country where—so the argument goes—wealth must come from increasing and more efficient mechanization. But eighteen million Indians feed themselves from the profits of their handlooms, a further five million earn their livelihood as craftsmen of a specifically Indian culture. How are they to coexist with the pressures of modern economics and lifestyles? And if this avenue of employment is closed, can India ever hope to create factory jobs for twenty-three million additional workers?

Perhaps the answer to such questions can still be found in mythology, because there is a happy ending to the myth about the spider goddess of the Indian subcontinent. Having trapped the foreign god of mechanization in her web, the goddess becomes mother, wife, and daughter to progress. Like the spinning goddess, Indian weavers have been the mother to Indian industry, the wife to Indian nationalism. The odds are they will succeed in becoming heirs to modern India's progress. They have done so in the past. The scientific developments that dealt the death blow to so much Indian culture have constantly reinforced India's textiles. The dyes used in the woven fragments that survive from the subcontinent's earliest archaeological remains—the Indus Valley civilization—are still the color spectrum that defines India: ocher, red, black, and the legendary indigo. Experiments in extracting color from plants led to the creation of these first dyes. Five thousand years later, experiments in re-creating this color palette chemically led to the growth of India's pharmaceutical industries.

As for mechanization, India's weavers have already absorbed some of the processes of the machine. But machines cannot duplicate an evolving world, and Indian weaving keeps abreast of Indian civilization only because the genius of India's weavers has proved great enough to contain that span.

The same knowledge that created the rich brocades worn by the Emperors of China and Byzantium creates the brocades worn by Indian brides and grooms today. The same skills which produced the "woven winds" worn by the Roman Emperors—those prized muslins which wrapped the body of the Buddha when he attained Nirvana and which were referred to by the Moghul Emperors as "morning dew" and "cloth of running water"—produce the muslins modern Indians wear in the punishing heat of summer. The same expertise that could weave wealth into beauty causes Indian brides today to preserve trousseaus woven with gold thread so that in time of necessity they can burn the fabric and sell the gold.

Painted fabrics that may not contain a single flaw in the weave are still hung seasonally in Indian temples, acts of devotion by master weavers. The Muslim weaver-embroiderers of northern India who weave the ninety-nine names of Allah into their work still see no contradiction in weaving brocade vestments worn by the Pope, regarding each textile as a form of prayer.

Waves of migrant weavers, displaced by industrialization, weave their homesickness into their fabrics, and those who buy them buy woven epics of dislocation. Tribal weavers use the brush and the loom to record the history of their travels, their work treasured by the anthropologist.

The knowledge of colors and cultures as they change with India's geography and peoples—the yellows of northern springs and wheat and mustard harvests, the whites and ivories of southern summers, the green of eastern rice fields and the seasons of desire, the old rose pinks and musk blues of Islam, the shades of indigo that denote the fury of the monsoon and the playful god of Brindaban, the differing shades of red that tell the varying constancies of lovers, the silvers and enameled golds of royalty—these are the raw materials of India's weavers. The designs and images that reinforce the meaning of colors and textures—these are the cultural province of India's weavers.

The paradox is this. Global mass production may seem an answer to poverty, but only a living culture can generate sustained wealth. There is a further paradox. If twenty-three million craftsmen depend on India's culture for their living, India's very culture depends on giving them a living. Without our craftsmen we would be indistinguishable from any other country, our unique multiplicities limited by the machine.

In the end, machines can only reproduce a culture, they can't invent one—and who is going to produce machines fast enough to reproduce the fabrics created by the encyclopedic knowledge, the endlessly changing adaptations of eighteen million weavers?

7

Food for Thought

I once saw a famine in the making. For three years the monsoon rains, life and death to rural India, had failed and there was drought in the state of Maharashtra. Crops had withered, livestock had starved, village wells were dry. By 1973, the third year of the drought, children were dying of hunger.

In the towns there was no power or running water. The reservoirs had sunk so low that when I arrived in Aurangabad, a city of two million people, there was only enough drinking water for two days. I found its residents preparing to join the exodus that had already clogged the roads leading to the state capital, Bombay—where one out of every seven people was living on the streets.

To halt the exodus, the government was tackling the situation on a military footing. Food donated from the overflowing granaries of the United States was being airlifted to remote villages. Milelong lines of bullock carts bearing kerosene drums filled with drinking water were trundling down the roads in the opposite direction from the refugees. A mill owner had opened kitchens across the state serving a diet of his own devising that contained enough protein and calories to sustain a human being for at least twenty-four hours. Famished villagers queued at his kitchens while government radio railed against their obstinacy in refusing American grain, to which their palates were unaccustomed.

One of India's most distinguished political cartoonists and I accompanied a district commissioner to a village in the epicenter of the drought. Sitting on the caked ground outside their huts, emaciated village women were sifting through the wheat piled in heaps by their sides. They shook their cane trays furiously in a kind of hypnotic rhythm like the sound of mariachis, oblivious to the wailing of their children. Every few seconds they would stop, pick a grain or two out of the tray, and put the grains to one side.

A bullock cart rolled to a stop on the outskirts of the village. The children stopped crying and crowded around the cart, holding out clay cups for water, cupping their hands to catch drops splashing from the cart onto the brown dust blowing across the ground. The women shouted at the children to fill the earthenware pots stacked outside the huts so that their fathers would have water to drink.

"Where are your husbands?" I asked the women, seeing no men in the village.

"Digging an irrigation canal."

"In a drought?"

"For the next rains, if they ever come. 'Food for Work,' the government officers call it. When our men build roads or dig canals, they are paid in food."

They shook their basket trays angrily. "Poisoned food."

The political cartoonist was sketching the white-turbanned farmer pulling at the bullock's horns to direct the animal back onto the road. The children deserted the cart to peer over his shoulder at the images forming on his white paper.

"Take my photograph!" they shouted, pushing each other out of the way to get closer to the artist, pleased to show off their knowledge of technology.

"Take my photograph too!"

"And mine!"

As he patiently drew quick sketches for the children, I watched the women monotonously sifting their grain, picking out seeds from the wheat and placing them carefully in containers.

I couldn't understand why the women were engaging in such fastidious preparation when their children were hungry. "Why don't you just cook it?"

"We don't want to die," they answered wearily.

"Look!" A woman held up a handful of the separated seeds so that I could see for myself. "Datura in the wheat."

Safe for animal consumption, poisonous to human beings—the grain donated by the United States was cattle feed.

Still, when you are starving, you take what you can get.

I, on the other hand, was being given more than I could possibly consume. Enough to keep ten families fed at every meal. Enough liquor to keep ten men intoxicated for a week. A private airplane to fly me around the state. Cars to drive me to the worst sites of the drought. I was working for a British television company, you see. The cartoonist shared my privileges. He was working for a British newspaper. Because of our foreign employers we were honorary foreigners, traveling with the foreign journalists. So we shared in all the luxuries by which we in the Third World seduce the First World into paying attention to our problems.

This business of trying to impress the First World has cost the Third World dearly.

In the thirties a European journalist once asked Mahatma Gandhi, "How can I understand India?"

"Study her villages," Gandhi replied. It was an obvious answer. After all, three quarters of India lived in villages.

But the West was wealthy from industry, and in the fifties Prime Minister Nehru and his advisers came up with a bold new plan to take India's bullock-cart economy into the machine age of the twentieth century. If America was building gigantic hydroelectric projects like the Boulder and Coulee dams, we would also build huge dams to provide power for our dream of mechanization. If Five Year Plans and state-controlled industry were the magic bullets of development used by China and Russia, we would also channel our resources into massive state-owned industries to create jobs. If every year we were importing food to stave off famine, then that was the price a poor country had to pay for progress. After all, we had always had famines.

It took a new Prime Minister, Shastri, to notice that our obsession with state industry was too expensive. More than factories, Indians needed to eat. Perhaps the fortunes we were borrowing to import food might be better spent helping Indian farmers to grow it. After all, in the vast sweep of the Indo-Gangetic Basin we had the most extensively cultivated alluvial plain in the world. Farther south we had the fertile volcanic soil of the great Deccan Plateau. Actually, we had as much cultivatable land as China without China's population, as well as a population density even today only slightly higher than Germany's, much lower than Japan's, leading the American Overseas Development Council to acknowledge that "India has a natural endowment for food production very close to that of the United States."

Prime Minister Shastri chose a propitious moment to turn India's focus back to agriculture. It was the sixties and world scientists had achieved a breakthrough in crop production—high-yielding hybrid seeds for wheat and rice, the two staple foods of Indians.

Everyone said it would take years of coaxing to make the cautious, backward, suspicious Indian farmer use them. Instead, newspapers were soon printing stories of burly Sikh farmers breaking into Punjab research laboratories in dead of night to steal the miracle wheat seeds and plant them before the next rains. In the

South scientists were complaining they had no more seeds with which to experiment because their rice samples had mysteriously vanished.

It was the beginning of the green revolution.

In the years that followed, the monsoons were still unpredictable. The rains still failed and we still had droughts. But within a decade we were able to feed ourselves. Another decade and we were exporting cereals. Ten years after that we were exporting a quarter of our agricultural produce. The green revolution had changed India forever.

Yet millions of Indians were still hungry, millions of dispossessed villagers were still migrating to the cities. We were spending fortunes on rural development, but more than half our water, our most precious resource, was being lost every year to floods and to evaporation caused by deforestation and mining and quarrying, while half our villages still had no drinking water.

A huge burst of effort was needed to consolidate our gains. Better irrigation, soil conservation, primary education, health facilities—these could change the face of rural India.

These—and effective land reforms. After all, we were a young nation of ancient inequalities where absentee landlords had owned vast hereditary holdings farmed by tenant farmers who paid a third of their produce to the landlord, another third to middlemen often doubling as moneylenders, leaving the farmers to pay for everything else while facing the constant threat of eviction.

But we were also the land of Mahatma Gandhi, and for twenty years Vinoba Bhave, a frail old man who had been one of Gandhi's closest associates, toured independent India urging landlords to donate land to the poor, reminding us that only the redistribution of land could give India's millions of landless laborers and tenant farmers a stake in the country's future.

Indeed, as early as 1951 Prime Minister Nehru's government had passed a resolution limiting the amount of land any individual could own. Farmers had to "personally" cultivate their fields and "accept the whole risk" of cultivation. Excess land would be bought by Government and sold cheap to tenant farmers who would form cooperatives to prevent fragmentation.

The resolution succeeded in redistributing feudal holdings—but not to debt-laden migrant workers or subsistence farmers. It was the moderately prosperous farmer, and the ubiquitous moneylender claiming he underwrote "the whole risk" who had the money to take advantage of the reforms—and of all the resources Government was pumping into the countryside.

As Mahatma Gandhi said, we should have studied our villages. But our city-bred planners did not do so, and now instead of being exploited by large landlords, our landless laborers were being exploited by small landlords, their condition deteriorating as the price of farming increased.

By the seventies urban India learned its errors. Rural India had become politically conscious.

In 1979 one million farmers marched on Delhi. Men from the North with rough blankets thrown over their shoulders. Sikh farmers in shiny tractors from what was being called the bread basket of the Punjab. Men with turbans and elaborate earrings from the harsh semidesert lands of Rajasthan; men wearing dhotis from the East; men with caste marks on their foreheads from the South. Water was their first demand. Then, seeds, fertilizers, electricity.

By 1980 the farmers weren't bothering to march on Delhi. They had launched nationwide movements, demanding higher prices for their crops. Our intimidated leaders responded by hastily borrowing money abroad so that they could give tax concessions to the farmers. Then they borrowed more money to keep the cost of food low so that the poor could eat. As populism took precedence over pragmatism, subsidies spiraled until the annual cost to the nation for subsidized fertilizers alone had jumped to over two billion dollars.

And like her landless laborers India was herself now in bondage, facing ever larger interest payments to her foreign creditors on ever larger loans.

But her poorest peasants, her migrant workers, her craftsmen dependent on diminishing village patronage, were still leaving the land.

For years we in the cities had thought the excitements of metropolitan life projected in glorious color through films and television were causing the rural migration. Too late we recognized that a neglected agricultural infrastructure was sending the dispossessed into town in search of work.

When I was a child, only fifty million Indians lived in the Indian cities; today four hundred million do, twice the population of the United States. Their numbers are threatening our urban infrastructure, and our bursting cities cannot contain them.

As our cities explode into the countryside, it is at last the turn of the peasant to patronize the urban Indian.

"For fifty years I worked this land," an old farmer remarked when the city of Delhi reached his mud hut and prospective real estate buyers descended on him, offering large sums of money for his unirrigated field.

"From before sunrise until after sunset I pulled the plough with my own shoulders because I didn't have enough money for a buffalo to till my field. I prayed for rain when the seeds were sown. I prayed for no rain when the plants were high. My wife collected cow dung for cooking fuel, and in good years we bartered our wheat at the price set by middlemen so we could send at least one son to school."

He sighed with pleasure. "Isn't it wonderful? I worked so hard for so many years, but the land gave me so little. Now I get up every morning and just smile at my field. And each day I get richer."

8

New Money

Anyone who doubts India is changing should cast a quick glance around our cities, home to our new and booming urban middle class.

Whole families dressed in shiny synthetic fabrics squash onto scooters driven by men with pomaded hair wearing shades and terylene trousers and those pointed shoes which used to be called "brothel-creepers."

Higher up the feeding chain there are gold watches, German cars, Italian clothes, yachts and airplanes, Cristal and Dom Pérignon champagnes, reserved tables for sprawling families in the most expensive restaurants and discotheques. An awful lot of caviar congealing uneaten in an awful lot of Lalique bowls signals the new Indian attitude. If you've got it, flaunt it.

In the old days if you had it, you hid it. We were a poor country and self-denial was solidarity.

I remember when we were undergraduates at Cambridge University we were allowed only the bare minimum of hard currency to cover our fees. But we didn't mind too much. We were still under the sway of Mahatma Gandhi's austerity—although Sarojini Naidu, the indomitable woman who was Gandhi's companion in so many of the great nonviolent adventures that ended the British Raj, had once observed that it cost Indians a lot to keep Gandhi poor.

Twenty years later, when our economy remained stuck at the dismal low dismissed disparagingly by our economists as the Hindu rate of growth, we would understand Sarojini Naidu's perspicacious comment. Then we would admit that the austerities enforced on us by the errors of central planning had proved even more expensive for the nation than Mahatma Gandhi's poverty.

But in the early sixties we seemed to have got our planning right. Analysts around the world were telling us that India was ready for economic take-off, and as undergraduates we could still afford to feel morally superior to the self-indulgence of our colleagues.

Especially our subcontinental colleagues at Cambridge. But then, reverse snobbery was our only option when the Pakistani government had no currency restrictions and the richest Pakistani students could show off their wealth. Oh, those wicked Pakistanis, so stylishly dressed by Anderson and Shepherd. Our penury limited us to a determined display of homespun modesty rather than dashing wardrobes from the most expensive Savile Row tailors. How else were we to make a virtue of our poverty except by adopting a stern Robespierreian disdain for the Danton-like sybarites from north of the subcontinental border?

They kept polo ponies. They smoked Havana cigars. They raced around in Lotus sports cars with headlights that went up and down like eyes winking invitingly, and a lot of pretty European girls studying English in local language schools took up those invitations—a lot more than ever accepted invitations from the impoverished Indian students.

Still, we did have one thing the flashy Pakistani students lacked. Our leader, the Prime Minister of India, was an Honorary Doctor of Cambridge University. Because of Nehru we affected contempt for what India's planners called "luxury goods." We would eschew luxury goods for cheap goods we could make ourselves. We would nationalize a lot of our industries. We would regulate what was left.

We would ignore the alarmed voices raised in India's Parliament against this ideological posturing. "A country that loses sixty percent of its water every year through mismanagement cannot afford ideology," the voices thundered. But we were living in the age of ideology, in the very heart of a cold war that pitted social justice against ruthless capitalism, and we wore our poverty with pride. After all, it was the heyday of Nehru's socialism. He had been honored by one of the most respected academies in the world. And he was One of Us.

Free of such enervating considerations, the Pakistani students continued to holiday on the French Riviera, driving from one modish resort to another. Our crushing exchange restrictions meant we couldn't go anywhere unless we were prepared to spend days standing by the side of highways with our thumbs tentatively extended, unconvincing hitchhikers.

Perhaps such humiliations led one of those impoverished Indian students, Rajiv Gandhi, to begin lifting currency restrictions when he became Prime Minister. Or perhaps it was the accumulation of further restrictions imposed on the country by his mother. Prime Minister Indira Gandhi had spent most of the seventies expanding government until it interfered in every aspect of Indian life. During her time in office the steep rise in world oil prices had sent the cost of Indian essential commodities soaring. Workers in the nationalized industries were striking for higher wages, rural India was demanding a larger share of resources.

But Mrs. Gandhi proceeded to nationalize insurance companies and banks. And her new restraints on private industry became so elaborate they assured a virtual monopoly to anyone who succeeded in actually obtaining an industrial license, even though the successful industrialist was still not allowed to produce to full capacity, only to a government quota. If the quota was too small and demand too great, black marketing filled the void, creating mountains of undeclared cash that could not be used to build more factories, grow more food, create more jobs.

An awed report in *The Economist* noted of our system, "This has no equal in the world. In many ways it puts Soviet central planning to shame."

Less charitably, our own economists said we had created the Land of the Permit License Raj.

It was all done for the best possible motives. Self-reliance. Independence from the Western commercial imperialism that had replaced Western political imperialism. But even when we were undergraduates, secretly envying our Pakistani colleagues, we suspected that something had gone wrong.

Still, it's never too late to right a wrong, and one of our contemporaries was finally doing something about it. Dismissing our hollow self-reliance, Rajiv Gandhi was opening up India's economy to the world, deregulating industry, slashing taxes.

What's more, he was taking a visible delight in those sinful imported items we had been denied so long. Like the Indian housewife in V. S. Naipaul's *Area of Darkness*, our new Prime Minister was "craze for foreign. Just craze for foreign." He wore imported aviator glasses and drove imported fast cars and drank imported mineral water. Where Nehru and Shashtri had traveled by commercial airlines, he was having a whole Boeing reappointed for his use, while the decorators who refurbished his home were themselves being decorated with government honors.

Watching him, we realized Homespun was Out, Luxury Goods were In.

After forty long years we could say good-bye to the hair shirt of poverty. For the first time in independent India it was politically correct to be rich.

9

An Embarrassment
of Riches

Delhi is among the fastest-growing cities in the world, but I think the census takers start their counting in the wintertime, when the city is overrun by hordes of Westerners fleeing the snow.

The foreigners who arrived in Delhi during the seventies came in search of spiritual enlightenment. Now it was the glorious eighties. Our Prime Minister, Rajiv Gandhi, was a young, good-looking baby boomer who was liberalizing the Indian economy. Money had become the new enlightenment.

So I wasn't surprised when a gentleman approached me at a dinner party. "Five hundred international Young Presidents and their wives are arriving for India 1986. We would like you to address them, give them a different picture of India that will encourage investment."

I looked solemn. The gravity of his demeanor suggested the approach of—well, what was a Young President?

"Financial and industrial dynamos. They all became heads of their own companies by the age of forty."

And what was India 1986?

"An attempt to get them to start companies here. The other speakers are Dr. Kissinger, Mother Teresa, and the Dalai Lama."

This was serious flattery—to be told your peers were a Star, a Saint, and a God. Mere patriotism paled into insignificance. But what do you say to Young Presidents when you have neither expertise nor sanctity on your side, and certainly not divinity? I had a few jokes. Was that enough to make these tigers of trade invest in India?

I rang headquarters, Young Presidents' Organization, New York. Brisk voices replied, conjuring up images of smart young things in uniforms pushing flagged figures of entrepreneurs around a map of the world.

"I don't want to come on after Mother Teresa," I said, appealing to their distant sympathy.

"Why not?"

"Nobody can follow Mother Teresa. It's like coming on after Little Richard."

"Oh, really? We'll fix it. Our literature is on its way. Have a good day."

The literature arrived, a curriculum appropriately bound in that luxurious crimson associated with Les Must de Cartier. Within it were photographs of a large number of speakers, and Dr. Kissinger and the Dalai Lama weren't among them. I had been conned by a Young President.

But my disappointment dissolved in the anticipation of hearing Ms. Bettina Arndt address five hundred corporate presidents on the theme NOT TONIGHT, DEAR, I HAVE A HEADACHE, followed perhaps too obviously by IS THE BOSS A LOUSY LOVER?

Boy, that should pull in a lot of investment for India.

Sandwiched between the editor of the *Washington Times*'s lecture on SOUTH AFRICA: RACE WAR OR MODUS VIVENDI? and the Porsche chairman's lecture on PLANNING AN INTERNATIONAL BUSINESS IN UNCERTAIN TIMES, someone was going to discuss the dilemma of "plateauing."

Plateauing?

Whatever plateauing meant, it was going to

be discussed in the lecture RESOLVING THE MIDLIFE CRISIS: INSIGHTS FROM INDIA. Could the speaker pull it off? I wondered. Midday Crises we could handle in India, even Midweek Crises. But had we clambered sufficiently high up the evolutionary ladder to qualify for Midlife Crises?

And my own lecture on the Westerners who had given up their expensive toys in the hope of acquiring India's fabled spiritual depth, while Indians traded anything they had, including spiritual depth, for the chance of owning those discarded toys—was it an illustration of such a crisis?

By the time the conference was to begin, the Prime Minister of India, our Foreign Secretary, our top advisers on planning and administrative reforms, were all on the agenda. A weight lifted from my shoulders. If they couldn't convince the entrepreneurs of the world to invest in India, who could? Unless the way to a president's heart was through his stomach, in which case we had as backup the five primary sauces of India to be demonstrated in a lecture on THE COLOURFUL WORLD OF INDIAN CUISINE: BROWN, RED, YELLOW, WHITE, AND GREEN.

And then the five hundred presidents and their wives were in town, snarling up the traffic, hogging the hotel rooms. Business as usual. Not so usual were the sideshows in the hotel foyers in homage to the one essential required for inclusion in the Young Presidents' Organization— Big Bucks. Jewelers bent over gems, peering through the loupes fixed to their eyes. Vendors who had come all the way from Varanasi smiled politely as they tried to slide fragile glass bangles over wrists larger than any they had ever seen. Veiled women from Rajasthan leaned over copper bowls filled with henna paste to paint elaborate fertility designs on the palms of queuing wives. Sometimes the ladies were joined by the Young Presidents themselves, but no one laughed during the conference when men proffered hands covered with female fertility designs. After all, the rich are supposed to be different.

The only person who hadn't grasped this was an astrologer seated like a pasha on cushions, surrounded by adoring Westerners as he ministered to future midlife crises.

I watched a personable young fruit-and-vegetable millionaire from Australia have his future told. He was surprised by the astrologer's accurate reading of his past, thrilled to learn that he hadn't yet plateaued.

"But greater success is yet to come," the soothsayer shouted in delight, staring at the horoscope he had cast. "You will change direction into new paths of great wealth. More remunerative than your present business even."

"What will I be doing?" the Australian millionaire inquired eagerly.

"Have no fears, sir. Soon you will become a, a . . ."

Twenty of us waited, holding our breath.

"A moneylender!" the astrologer announced triumphantly, dismissing fruit-and-vegetable fortunes as slim pickings compared to the wealth to be had from loan-sharking, which lifted a man into the rarefied world inhabited by the truly rich.

Actually, what identified these rich was their sheer stamina. From dawn jogging and yoga classes via a quick swim and a set of tennis, they raced off to learn how to tie saris and turbans, drove a hundred miles to Agra to see the Taj Mahal, bought carpets, were received for tea by a real President—the President of India—watched polo matches played by the Sixty-first Cavalry Regiment, visited outlying factories and villages, dined in different houses to see how real Indians lived, shopped ceaselessly, and still managed to attend the lectures taking place throughout the day. And they were in town only for a week.

The crisp voices from New York, in person

belonging to people more *Cosmopolitan* than Third Reich, remained maddeningly unflappable as they orchestrated solutions to all this busywork and other India '86 problems. I complained that now I was following not only Mother Teresa but the Prime Minister as well. What kind of billing was that? The organizers clucked sympathetically, didn't change a thing, and gave me a sandalwood medallion engraved with my name and designation—FACULTY—and a cloth satchel filled with that glossy paper that sticks to your fingers. More crimson brochures that listed the best eating and shopping in India, proliferating proof of the twentieth century's drive to consume.

At least that's what Mother Teresa implied in her shockingly contemporary appeal. She wanted help for victims of AIDS. The Young Presidents had already agreed to ante up a million tax-deductible dollars for her hospices in New York. Now she was telling them their money wasn't good enough. She wanted their personal participation, volunteers to work with the patients. The haze of sentimentality evaporated instantly. No one was prepared to extend a hennaed hand in lieu of a checkbook. Easier to accommodate was her request that they be humane to their employees—inquire about children's names.

The Young Presidents knew what to call each other. Apart from the sandalwood medallions hanging around their necks, there was a crimson book titled *Who's Here*, giving their names and then—their nicknames. Wiping tears of emotion from their eyes as Mother Teresa ended her address, the Eds, Bobs, Als, Chucks, married to the Babses, Frans, Connies, Sues, settled back in their chairs to listen to the next speaker—a man who could have been one of their own.

Head of a country by the age of forty, the open-minded Prime Minister of India was telling them how he wanted to take his unwieldy corporation into the twenty-first century. Just as Mother Teresa was the acceptable face of charity, so Rajiv Gandhi was the acceptable face of Third World leadership.

When he had left, everyone filled in their evaluation forms. There were six categories and eight subcategories by which all speakers— saints, Prime Ministers, geopolitical experts— were to be judged. One was the lowest rating, ten the highest. Rajiv Gandhi made only Sixes and Sevens. Mother Teresa was a straight and unanimous Ten. After all, she was a Star.

And Stars are for consumers. As Mother Teresa tried to make her getaway, she was hauled out of her van by millionaires pleading to be photographed with her. Looking like an irritated E.T. in her white sari with its blue border, she reluctantly dismounted from her van again and again. But she was consoled when she heard her score.

"I'm a Ten! I'm a Ten!" she crowed to her nuns. "What does that mean?"

"You're the new Bo Derek!" said friends who had worked with her from the time she had begun her mission. The younger nuns, just in from the world, giggled knowingly when the friends promised to bring her a video of the movie so that she could see what a Ten really was.

Things are seldom what they seem. These movers and shakers from the West who were devouring India like great white sharks also had another persona capable of delving deeper into the subcontinent. At the end of every lecture they asked highly informed questions about Indian political and economic matters. When had they found the time to think about such things? That whole week in crowded conference halls, global infobabble had seeped from under closed doors. To be a dynamo in today's world, did you need a capacity to simply absorb information like a human floppy disk in order to generate wealth?

It was a mystery. Almost as mysterious as the

closing spectacular of India '86. "Destination Secret," said the invitation. "Black Tie." And the next day they would all be gone.

Young millionaires who had brought canned food against India's many diseases distributed them to the surprised Delhi University students who had been their guides. Then the turban and sari experts arrived. For two hours turbans were wound onto the heads of the presidents, saris pleated around the waists of the more daring ladies. Clapping enthusiastically at their costumes, they made their way to the hotel foyer in anticipation of Destination Secret.

Suddenly a fanfare of trumpets cleared a path through one thousand cheering guests. Nodding graciously, a clutch of India's ex-rulers dressed in royal garb made their way through the crowd and down the marble hotel steps to mount the vintage Bentleys and Rolls-Royces lined up behind the horse carriages and caparisoned elephants that were to lead the procession to Destination Secret.

The millionaires joined the procession, clambering into palanquins borne by liveried bearers, or onto camels or horses. Or they walked so that they could better enjoy the spectacle of the avenue guarded by Gurkha soldiers standing in front of the hundreds of cummerbunded torchbearers holding lanterns. Thus, piped by Indian wedding bands, watched by gawping locals, we sashayed out of the front gates of the hotel to Destination Secret—which turned out to be the back gate of the same hotel.

Lining the approach to the back gate were mounted lancers. Beautiful young girls dressed in traditional red and ocher long skirts were flinging jasmine garlands at the ladies, marking the foreheads of the presidents with red powder, and spraying everyone in sight with scented rose water. To our left, a full military band, white uniforms bright against the dark lawns, was playing viceregal tunes as the ex-royals preceded the entrepreneurs into a Moghul tent for champagne cocktails. It was a fabulous finale. Every element of India—Moghul Empire, British Raj, traditional Hindu, contemporary wedding, erstwhile Maharajah, rather like the five primary sauces of Indian cuisine—had been reproduced to please the jaded palates of the Young Presidents. And perhaps attract investment.

The banging of an enormous brass gong, followed by the cries of *"Hoshiar! Hoshiar!"*—once used by eunuchs to inform the harem that the ruler approached—alerted us to drain our champagne glasses and follow the Maharajahs into the banquet hall.

At dinner our silver platters were constantly

replenished with kebabs, curries, Indian breads, vegetables, our glasses filled to the brim with wines, champagnes, liqueurs, to keep us busy until the band came on.

Then for four hours an Indian dance band played the kind of music the Young Presidents must have loved, because the crowded dance floor couldn't take any more financial dynamos and they were jiving in the aisles.

The gentleman on my left, a cabinet minister from the royal Thai government, observed laconically that just that morning he had been addressing these demon dancers on the issue of population control in the Third World.

"By the way, do you have a key chain?" he asked. As I rummaged in my handbag, I could hear one of the Young Presidents on the microphone crooning "Feelings" to his applauding colleagues.

"Sorry. I'm not carrying any keys."

The cabinet minister reached into his elegantly cut dinner jacket and produced one. I examined it. There was a plastic bubble in the center of the key chain. Over the bubble was printed the instruction IN CASE OF EMERGENCY BREAK GLASS. The minister lifted a candle so that I could see more clearly. Under the bubble was—an electric blue condom.

Someone pulled me from my chair to join the

singers. Was this an emergency? Would an electric blue condom help? Or should I save my key chain in case I was invited to address next year's conference?

India '86 was already over. On the dance floor they were holding hands and singing the theme song of the African famine, "We are the world, we are the children."

According to the brochure of the Young Presidents' Organization, "If you liked the movie *Out of Africa* you are going to love Africa '87."

10

Typing

"It's a scandal!" the French intellectual said with a passion available only to energetic Westerners. I looked around the bazaar nervously and saw small boys in torn short pants kicking flimsy plastic shopping bags across a dirty courtyard.

The year was 1996 and we were in one of those shopping complexes that have burgeoned all over the major Indian cities—hideous structures made of unpainted concrete, red streaks of betel juice marking their chipped steps.

The stench of badly cured leather competed with the smell of fast food being fried in corner cafés where customers had stopped for snacks after renting their evening's entertainment from video shops. Racks of garments that couldn't be crammed into the tiny shops collected dust in crowded corridors, next to rows of shoes piled in precarious pyramids. Loud film music emanated from record stores, drowning civilized conversation, disturbing the students pounding away at their rented keyboards in their computer course schools consisting of two tables, two chairs, two machines.

"What is a scandal?" In the presence of so many possibilities, I was unable to identify the target of her anger.

"These videos!" she hissed, waving at the garish poster of an Indian film taped to the window of a store. I examined the poster. It had a certain vitality, putting me in mind of the Indian hotel that advertised a stripper's attractions with the headline COME AND SEE. CRUDE AND VIVACIOUS GWENDOLINA. Surely even a French intellectual was not going to demand aesthetics in an Indian bazaar.

"Do you know what these video people are doing?" she persisted angrily, and I felt something bad was coming. "They have put religious rituals on film! Imagine switching on a machine so your priest can chant prayers while you prostrate yourself in front of the television."

I stared at her in blank relief. She waved an

embroidered muslin shirt at me, outraged at my obstinate stupidity. "But just think. People are *worshipping* their videos!"

What's the big deal? I thought to myself. Worshipping videos? Get a grip. This is India. We worship air conditioners and computers and cash registers and bullock carts—in an annual ritual called Weapon Worship.

For millennia Indians have believed man is distinguished from his fellow animals by his capacity for making tools. By honoring our implements, we honor human ingenuity, and Weapon Worship originated with warriors honoring their weapons, the tools of their trade. In modern India people still place garlands on the machines of their differing trades, hoping for an auspicious response. Actually, any response at all will do, so on the day of Weapon Worship, machines are offered coconuts, smeared with vermilion, propitiated by so many sticks of incense that they disappear into clouds of scented smoke.

In our electronic age new machines are arriving with such velocity, honoring them can take more than just a day. Only a handful of years ago we were not allowed to import color television sets. Today color televisions are made in the country. Indian-made computers, fax machines, telephone answering machines, and all the other paraphernalia of instant communications are making it possible for Indians to be part of the future.

A few years ago our telephone system could only be described as disastrous, available just in cities to people prepared to queue for years or pay hefty bribes. Now public telephones in the countryside are freeing the farmer of the scourge of rapacious middlemen, enabling him to establish the market price for his own crops.

The handheld cellular telephone, that appendage of the successful urbanite, has even made its entry into parts of rural India. Sometimes you can see a villager lying on his perennial string bed outside his mud-and-stone house, a bullock or two tethered in the background, near an Indian car parked under the shade of a tree. The villager himself will be drawing on a hookah and talking into a cellular phone, possibly making a real estate deal as the city's boundaries stretch toward his fields. Or he may be establishing crop prices from the grain market. Or he may be hiring an Indian-made tractor.

The surging energy gathering momentum in India is visible on our crowded city streets. When did so many Indians buy those cars which they drive so dangerously, with those awful car horns which they lean on from the moment they switch on the ignition? What are all those Benetton shops doing next to those sari shops, those Coca-Cola ads next to those ads for freeze-dried spices? Are those cyber cafés opening next to kebab restaurants? Is this the conspicuous consumption which we have so long abhorred? Or is this the new India framed by the old India, determined to take advantage of the breaks that are coming her way.

Those breaks took a long time coming, stifled by decades of steady encroachment by the state, until an economic impasse in the nineties forced the reforms that are finally releasing India's immense commercial energies. You have only to turn on an Indian-made television set to see the huge increase in goods now available to the consumer, only to open the morning newspaper in any city to see how many foreign investors are prepared to grapple with India's Byzantine rules to get their feet on the first rung of the ladder of India's impending economic boom.

Once it was the dream of educated Indians to be hired by government—government jobs meant a steady income and no one was ever fired. The dreams are changing. A feeling is in the air: government jobs are going to get leaner and less secure, while the private sector is expanding and paying higher salaries.

There used to be a joke about the state of

Kerala, which produces a vast number of government clerks because it has the highest literacy rate in the country. Its politically conscious population are often communists.

So someone asks a person from Kerala, "Are you a capitalist or a Marxist?"

"I'm a typist," he replies.

No one wants to be a typist anymore. The ugly Indian shopping complexes were once crammed with one-room typing schools. Now they are bursting with computer schools, evidence of the hunger for learning and self-improvement that typifies the Indian.

Indians are nothing if not canny. They can sense that the wind is now blowing from another direction, and that there's money to be had in the change. Five years ago only five thousand Indians were working in computers. Today a quarter of a million Indians are busy producing computer software that is used around the world, bought by the Fortune 500 companies. Tomorrow electronics might well employ five hundred thousand people—our youngest industry is also among our fastest growing, already exporting a billion dollars in electronic goods abroad.

It has been said that what his Western counterpart demands as a right is seen by the Indian as an opportunity. And for nearly two centuries we have known that opportunity and communications are inseparable. Communications conquered us—the telegraph, the train, the constantly communicating bureaucracy of the British Raj. We were avid to own them, and when the British left, from four major universities the number of Indian universities jumped to over ninety. The average number of students grew until today each of our largest universities, in Calcutta and Delhi, Madras and Bombay, have over a hundred thousand students, and annually turn away twice that number in applicants. Five million Indians graduate from university each year, and technological training institutes generate a steady stream of scientists and engineers.

Yet too many Indians still cannot read a name or write a number, a huge brake on our hopes of future development. Today over ninety percent of South Koreans are fully literate; fifty percent of Indians are illiterate—a result of Prime Minister Nehru's concentration on higher education, and the third Five Year Plan under Indira Gandhi, which did not give literacy high priority, although literacy produces a rise in the standard of living and a corresponding plunge in population.

To the great relief of the poor, primary education has finally become our top planning priority. Poverty is a state of mind as well as an economic condition, a hopelessness, a knowledge that things can never change. Any chink in that bleak wall of despair and the poor are the first to race through it. For them it is a matter of life or death. Ask any Indian villager what he wants and the reply is always "an education for my children." Ask any indigent Indian living in a town or city what he wants and the answer is invariably the same.

Those who are not so poor share the same passion. Today the pressure for school and university places is such that children as young as three years old have to take an examination before they can even get into nursery school. Lampposts and trees in Indian towns carry advertisements from people offering themselves as tutors. Parents are prepared to pay huge sums of money known as capitation fees, but which are actually bribes by a prettier name, to guarantee their children a place in private schools and colleges. I once met the president of America's most prestigious business school, who had been to India on a holiday. He was overwhelmed by the number of parents who located him in his various hotel suites, demanding, begging, pleading for their children's admission.

The skills of the modern world are by no means alien to us. Doctors, engineers, laboratory workers, economists, accountants—at the level of medium technology, Indians are second to none. And each time there is a new advance in technology, Indians are ready to seize it.

And when Silicon Valley in California sleeps, Indian scientists wake up in what is being called the Silicon Valley of Asia, the Indian city of Bangalore, to address the same problems that their sleeping American colleagues tried to solve the previous day, taking advantage of the electronic phenomenon that enables knowledge to be exchanged on a twenty-four-hour basis on the information superhighway.

Some might ask why there isn't a bigger brain drain from India today. Many Indian scientists reply that they do not want to lose a world of close family relationships and festivals. A world where religious ceremonies can safely be transferred onto videotape. Where newspapers, describing the popularity of televised mythologies, can safely carry the headline GODS WORK.

Ancient pragmatisms are India's saving grace, preserving a way of life in which the machine is still used by man, not one in which man becomes his machine. But that is a difficult thing to explain to someone from the West. Which is why the angry French intellectual saw electronic worship as a scandal and I saw it as a celebration.

For me the real scandal was that four hundred million Indians still had no machines to worship.

11

Dreaming

It is so dispiriting to be an Indian reading about Malaysia, South Korea, Singapore, Thailand, Indonesia. With their booming economies our neighbors are called the Southeast Asian Tigers. To my chagrin, India is usually described by analysts around the world as the Caged Tiger, a country that has yet to exploit its enormous potential.

And then I read these comparisons between India and China. India is always the elephant, China the hare.

And then a banker rings me from London. He is analyzing the Indian market.

"Is it true that India has twenty million dollar millionaires?" he asks reverently.

The meter ticks expensively as the banker

and myself silently consider the implications of the question. Twenty million of us? Dollar millionaires? Could such a thing be possible? Who are these millionaires anyway? How did they make their money?

I guess some got rich from the flourishing black market that our government controls created by "protecting the poor." Some were the kings of the Permit License Raj, monopolizing the very industries government restrictions were designed to prevent them from monopolizing. Some were stock brokers who inflated the markets out of all proportion because too many industries were nationalized, leaving too much cash chasing too few company shares. Some owed their wealth to the value of their houses in the bursting and ill-planned Indian metropolises, where today real estate is more expensive than in New York or London.

And many, far too many, had once been poor politicians and bureaucrats.

But the poorest Indian is still poorer than his counterpart in sub-Saharan Africa. It should not be so. With our thrift as a people, our technical manpower, our stable administration, we had the resources to become an economic tiger long ago. Alas, busy drawing maps for our lives with the same high-handedness with which nineteenth-century Europe had once drawn maps of our geography, our political leaders had ensured that a country with four times the population of America was producing the same amount of goods as Holland.

They need only have looked around the world to see the obvious. Outside the restrictions of their own country, Indians who live abroad are a blur of economic activity. Why can't we do the same at home? Why can't we produce more than Holland?

But one Indian Prime Minister after another, in the attempt to remove poverty, had only mired us further in it.

In the fifties Nehru had dreamt of a self-sufficient economy through rapid industrialization and neglected the needs of rural India.

The gains of the green revolution of the sixties were lost in the seventies to obsessive centralization and spiraling farm subsidies.

In the eighties, Rajiv Gandhi's interest in a new India was soon exchanged for the political maneuverings of the old India, while his successor, V. P. Singh, was less concerned with economic development than with political change.

By the nineties it was too late to ignore the economy. We had never defaulted on our debts. Now our foreign currency reserves were so depleted that the nation's gold was sent to London as surety against international loans. The world's credit agencies immediately demanded that India reduce her public sector, cut subsidies to agriculture, reform the tax structure.

In 1991 Prime Minister Rao undertook the delicate balancing act of moving the creaking machinery of Indian socialism toward a market economy.

Now India stands on the brink of a new millennium and "Growth" and "Opportunity" have become the new Indian slogans. Can they bend the bars that keep India caged? Can we sprint past China's hare?

Look at what we have going for us. Two hundred fifty million Indians are part of a still growing middle class. On top of that, four hundred million Indians can purchase essentials. That's an awful lot of clothes and cooking utensils. Even with our creeping rate of growth, we already possess a marketplace of half a billion people. Increase it and we could double our middle class, make it possible for every Indian to purchase essentials. Then we would have a marketplace of nearly a billion people, and from twenty million dollar millionaires today, we could have ten times that number tomorrow. Two hundred million dollar millionaires. More than in the United States. In fact, as many dollar millionaires as there are Americans.

There is really nothing to stop us. Unless political opportunism, the dread mistress of Indian economics, exacts her usual price.

But democracy is a time bomb and we are the largest democracy in the world. We are also, as the writer V. S. Naipaul said, the land of a million mutinies now.

12

Writing

In the 1890s, when the terrible cruelty of the caste system was still denying education to millions of Indians, the ruler of Baroda, one of India's largest kingdoms, made education free for all castes.

In ancient India castes had been like guilds, merely describing a man's occupation. Though belonging to the lowest caste, the sage Vyasa had compiled India's epic religious poem, the *Mahabharata*, while the son of a low-caste woman had created the glorious Mauryan Empire. Indeed, when his grandson, Emperor Asoka, converted to Buddhism, Asoka's great universities had disseminated the Buddha's teachings until they became the religion of Asia.

But over millennia caste had somehow degenerated until a man's occupation became an immutable fact of birth. The lowest caste of scavengers and refuse collectors were treated as anathema, polluting other castes by their very shadows. They were called untouchables.

Death was the sentence to an untouchable who wanted an education. The Laws of Manu, followed by orthodox Hindus, prescribed the method of execution. If an untouchable even overheard Sanskrit, the language of the scriptures, he was to be killed by having molten lead poured into his ears.

In Baroda, allowed education at last, a young untouchable boy studied so hard he was able to acquire a bachelor of arts degree from Bombay University. Then he got a scholarship to Columbia University in New York. Leaving the United States as a doctor of philosophy, he went on to London University and gained a doctor of science degree.

Twice over, the untouchable boy achieved the impossible. He became Dr. Ambedkar.

Back in India, Mahatma Gandhi was insisting that untouchables be called Harijans—Children of God. But Dr. Ambedkar knew that an untouchable by any other name was still the detritus of a religion, the living hell from which Hindus hoped to liberate themselves through good acts to be acknowledged in rebirths higher up the ladder of reincarnation.

Determined to change a vast continent where nearly one third of the population was exploited by caste discrimination, he took another degree in London, this time in law.

In 1946 a committee was formed to write India's constitution, and by 1947 Dr. Ambedkar was its chairman.

During the four long years it took to draft the constitution, the subcontinent was convulsed by change. The British were departing. Five hundred independent rulers were merging their kingdoms into India and Pakistan—the eastern and western halves of Pakistan separated from each other by a thousand miles of India. The day after the two new nations of India and Pakistan became free, Britain announced its dreaded Partition awards and the subcontinent erupted in carnage as Hindus, Muslims, and Sikhs fled their ancestral homes in one of the largest migrations in human history, which would, in a single year, leave a million dead, seven million homeless.

And through all this raging turbulence, work on the Indian constitution continued.

To assist him in drafting the constitution, Dr. Ambedkar had at his disposal not just the constitutions of the Western world but ancient India's great work on the science of government—the *Artha Shastra*, attributed to Kautilya, a minister in the court of the Mauryan Empire.

He also had at his disposal history. On the third and final reading of the bill to enact the Indian constitution into law, Dr. Ambedkar noted, "It is not that India did not know what Democracy is. There was a time when India was studded with republics.

"It is not that India did not know Parliaments or Parliamentary Procedure. The Sanghas [Buddhist monastic orders] had rules regarding seating arrangements, rules regarding Motions, Resolutions, Quorom, Whip, Counting of Votes, Voting by Ballot, Censure Motion, Regularisation, Res Judicata, etc. . . . borrowed from the Political Assemblies functioning in the country at the time.

"This democratic system India lost. Will she lose it a second time?

"If we wish to maintain democracy not merely in form but also in fact . . . we must observe the caution which John Stuart Mill has given all those who are interested in the maintenance of democracy, namely, not to lay their liberties at the feet of even a great man, or to trust him with powers which enable him to subvert their institutions.

"Hero-worship is a sure road to degradation and to eventual dictatorship."

The Sovereign Republic of India was formally proclaimed on January 26, 1950, governed by a constitution that guaranteed:

The State shall not deny to any person equality before the law.

The State shall not discriminate against any citizen on grounds of religion, race, caste, sex.

"Untouchability" is abolished and its practise in any form is forbidden.

Now India prepared to go to the polls for her first general election. On that great occasion the untouchable lawyer who had drafted her constitution reminded the people of India that it was only a piece of paper until it was inscribed on the hearts of her citizens.

13

The Voice
of the People

For sheer idiosyncractic panache the spectacle of Indian democracy is unique. Where else would a hundred thousand naked sadhus with matted hair break off their meditations and descend from their mountain caves to scale the towering gates of the Indian Parliament, locked against a squirming wall of holy men waving iron tridents, determined to breach the nation's citadel and ban cow slaughter.

Where else would a mass of hermaphrodites and eunuchs dressed in brilliantly colored saris and weighted down with jewels march on the capital to demonstrate against family planning—on the grounds that it would statistically lessen their odds of being born.

Such displays suggest that the concept of nationhood we took so unthinkingly from nine-teenth-century Europe is too constricting for our diversity. But half a century after we ceased to be a colony, we still bristle with the oversensitive antennae of a colonized people vainly struggling to become a European nation state.

And Indian politicians assume that, individually, they alone can define such a nation state because only they know the "true Indian masses." Fortunately, the true Indian masses enjoy proving otherwise—a discovery made by our first Prime Minister when he toured the tribal areas of northeastern India.

The populations of these hill tracts often demonstrate against the cutting down of their forests by lumber contractors who contribute heavily to political coffers. Yet any representative who goes to Delhi to plead the tribal cause ends up in what the Prime Minister of India believes to be the zenith of tribal ambition—a photo opportunity with the nation's leader wearing some strange tribal headdress in jaunty solidarity.

So a number of press photographers were accompanying Prime Minister Nehru when he made a much publicized visit to the northeastern hills in 1957. As the airplane circled the valley, between the beautiful but increasingly denuded wooded hills, several hundred tiny figures could be seen waiting—tribals who had journeyed from their inaccessible homelands to greet the Prime Minister.

There were chiefs with huge headdresses of feathers and beads and horns, like dignified lines of Eastern Montezumas. Young women with long black hair cascading down their backs. Tribal matrons with woven shawls and sarongs. Handsome younger men with smooth, hairless faces and elegantly slanted eyes, lithe bodies visible under the stiff tribal cloths that covered one muscled shoulder, leaving the other bare, free to handle a spear or a bow.

The airplane landed, a great white bird with the symbol of the Indian nation, Emperor Asoka's pillar of truth, blazoned on its side. Would the childlike tribals be frightened by this miracle of aerodynamics descending from the heavens with its cargo of democratic divinity. Would they run for cover? But no, they were standing steady under quivering headdresses watching aircraft personnel leap out to fix the steps for the Prime Minister's descent and press photographers push forward for a clear view through their lenses.

Finally the great man himself appeared—to be received by a reverence so profound that even the accompanying journalists were silenced. Possessing a sense of history, the leader solemnly descended the aircraft steps, assuming this warlike people wished to give him a colorful guard of honor.

I suppose they did. Because as soon as he was on terra firma, they all turned with regimental precision and lifted their colorful sarongs. The Prime Minister of India found himself taking the salute of hundreds of naked tribal behinds.

14

Management Crisis

Modern India is a fiction.

A fiction in search of an administration.

The visions of an older generation—freedom, equality, nonviolence—have over fifty years been turned into siren songs by what the Indian writer Nirad Chaudhuri called the Continent of Circe. He chose an apt name for India: her political seductions have truly made swine out of men. And women.

It's the scale of India, you see. In 1911, when George V came to Delhi for his coronation as King Emperor, even he was impressed by the magnificence of his representative. Indeed, one Viceroy of India had observed, "The Emperor of China and I rule half the world and still have time for tea."

Increasingly, India's political leaders are finding tea and monarchy more palatable than governance. I suppose the reflected power of such a giant land creates megalomania in her elected representatives. Democracy may demand accountability, but when you are received by crowds of half a million, it's hard to believe you are accountable to anyone. Megalomania is also a convenient retreat from the alarming speed with which India is changing.

Partially, it is politics. Indians are no longer prepared to endure the injustices of the past. And living in a democracy, they are prepared to do something about it.

Partially, it is economics. In fifty years we have not yet found a system of development that meets the needs of both our vociferous population and a world of exploding scientific and financial expansion.

The chaos is enough to intimidate anyone. Rather than undertake the duties of their office, our leaders have too often settled for redefining the privileges of office, making political corruption so endemic that winning an election in India today is tantamount to winning a lottery for the family.

We are even pilloried by satirists for having a hereditary democracy while Britain makes do with a constitutional monarchy.

Still, from the vantage of time it is possible to see patterns leading us from the constitutional dreams of Dr. Ambedkar and the incorruptible nonviolent politics of Mahatma Gandhi to our present condition.

PART THREE

15

Last Rites

I had just turned five years old when I found myself attending my first political event. The cold January day had started normally enough. My brother and I were playing under a winter sun in the garden of our house in Delhi, while our parents chose to sit in the verandah listening to the large wooden radio.

We never listened to the radio, only watched it, fascinated by the bronze netting that vibrated with the resonance of the broadcast. But this afternoon my father suddenly shouted "No!" with such force the servants came out to see what was happening. We ran to the verandah to find Mother crying. To our surprise the servants were weeping too. Over the crackle of the radio the announcer repeated that Mahatma Gandhi had been shot three times and killed.

We were so small we were not quite sure who Mahatma Gandhi was, or even whether he was human or one of India's many deities. Later we learned he had been shot by a Hindu fanatic as he was preparing to leave on a peace march for the killing fields of Partition, where millions of people, uprooted by the map drawing of the British Empire that had given birth to the two nations of India and Pakistan only six months earlier, were still fleeing the orgy of fear and savagery that already had left a million Hindus and Muslims and Sikhs slaughtered in its wake.

After all this time I cannot remember the exact sequence of events, only that Father rushed to the house where the Mahatma had been shot. Mother, too distraught to leave home, insisted the servants take us with them to watch the Mahatma's body being taken to the funeral pyre.

Wondering what the excitement was about, we ran beside the servants toward the road where Gandhi's funeral cortege was expected. The pavements were already crowded with people standing four rows deep. It was a most unIndian crowd. There was no noise. Everyone had changed into white, the Indian color of mourning that was no color at all. There was no pushing or shoving, as if the whole city were frozen and one man's death bore evidence to the horror and the savagery that, overnight, had turned a city of half a million people into a city of two million as refugees poured in from the carnage of Partition.

I recall sitting on someone's shoulder, looking over the mass of heads, not scared in a crowd that newspapers with black bands around them, to signify a nation in mourning, would later estimate at a million and a half people.

In silence we watched the lorry bearing the Mahatma's body slowly approaching. It was crowded with bareheaded old people dressed in white, sitting uncomfortably wherever they could find a perch. At the top of the lorry was a mound covered with flowers. Only a small exposed head revealed this to be the corpse of the Mahatma, the first dead body I had ever seen. As it passed in front of us, mourners broke ranks in that silent crowd to step forward and throw flowers in its path, raising their voices to bless Gandhi, *"Amar rahe"*—"Stay immortal."

In a few hours there would be nothing left of the Mahatma but ashes, and on the radio the Prime Minister would announce to the nation, "The light has gone out of our lives."

When I grew older I learned the names of some of the old people riding on the lorry, and realized I had watched a human pageant of those who had fought for India's freedom taking the symbol of that freedom movement to his funeral pyre.

Then, I had seen only a mound covered with marigold garlands. It was not a frightening sight, and it certainly wasn't glamorous. Even as very small children we could feel the heavy-heartedness, the dignity of the occasion—somehow more real because it was so shabby. Just a lorry, a corpse circled by people weeping silently, watched by grieving Indians who knew that independent India, only six months old, had already lost her innocence.

Years later I saw Richard Attenborough's film *Gandhi*. In the film Gandhi's funeral cortege was a huge military affair, with gun carriages and serried rows of soldiers marching with slow and solemn precision to the beat of funereal drums. Wondering if my own memories could have been so warped by time, I asked one of the Mahatma's grandsons about the vast gap between my recollection and what I had seen on celluloid.

"Briefly, that ceremony did take place," he admitted. "Even though Gandhi-ji never wanted a production made of his death. It was invented by Nehru and Mountbatten. For the record."

What record? I wondered. Soldiers? Gun

carriages? For the disciple of nonviolence? All those uniforms and all that gold braid for the man who dared to wear a loincloth to his meeting with the King Emperor of India?

If ever anything would have been abhorrent to Gandhi, smacking of the very colonialism he had done everything in his power to end, it would have been the idea of a state funeral.

Yet in one of the most imperious grand gestures of the twentieth century, Gandhi had insisted that Lord Louis Mountbatten, the last British Viceroy of India, be invited by Indians to become our first head of state. It was an eccentric demand, but consistent. Indeed, for years Gandhi had seen no reason to expel the British from India.

"If they can govern justly," he had argued in the middle of a freedom movement, "what difference does it make?"

He changed his mind only after the limited self-government Britain had promised India did not materialize and the Empire refused to lift the tax on salt in a continent where the people needed salt to live. Stating that he now believed Britain incapable of just government, Gandhi wrote to the British Viceroy, "On bended knee I asked for bread and you gave me stone instead."

Then he embarked on his famous Salt March to the sea to make illegal salt—the nonviolent movement of civil disobedience that would dislodge the British Raj.

By inviting Mountbatten to become free India's first head of state, Gandhi wanted to dispel the nation's hatred of her past colonial masters. He was indifferent to Mountbatten's race. Gandhi never doubted the equality of all human beings. He wanted justice. That was why he could wear a loincloth to Buckingham Palace. But his death became an opportunity for Mountbatten and Nehru to show the world how well they could do state occasions.

I guess I was lucky. Even if he was dead, even if I was hardly more than a baby, I saw the actual Mahatma. Not a Mahatma invented for history or politics or films.

Alas, poor Gandhi.

Who had pleaded that the Indian National Congress was a freedom movement, not a political party, and should be disbanded when India became free.

Who had showed us that nonviolence and a proud humility went hand in hand.

Who had believed that Indians would govern themselves with greater justice than their colonial masters.

He did not even reach his funeral pyre before his luck ran out.

16

Finding the Center

When I attended Bombay University, the college at which I was a resident student was run by nuns—satisfying two requirements for my mother's peace of mind. The necessity for higher education. The necessity for stern chaperonage.

Although now a convent, by bizarre circumstance the college had originally housed the harem of the Maharajah of Indore, and his frowning visage still crowned the pink stucco pillars, watching disapprovingly as we convent girls carried on the way convent girls do, even though the nuns did their best to control our high spirits.

So, naturally, when I saw the sign up on the college bulletin board prohibiting all students from going to a particular area of the city because of a huge demonstration expected that afternoon, I immediately caught the next bus to the forbidden. It was my first opportunity to participate in a serious political event.

The demonstration was a key moment in India's democratic development. Kerala, our southernmost state—with the highest literacy rate in the country—had in a free and fair election voted for a communist government. Inexplicably, Prime Minister Nehru had overruled the election, although the right of every state in the republic to choose its own government was enshrined in our constitution. In fact, the Indian states had considerable autonomy from the central government in Delhi except in times of "emergency," and there had been no emergency.

The thought of India's constitution being betrayed by Nehru was inconceivable to us. He had spent years in British jails demanding democracy. When we achieved democracy, Nehru had led the National Congress party to victory in three successive elections. All our conscious lives, he was the only Prime Minister we had ever known. He had encouraged us to call him Uncle Nehru, improved the homespun look of Mahatma Gandhi with a perennial rosebud in his coat, and kept tiger cubs in the gardens of the beautiful prime ministerial residence.

True, he had recently shown an Achilles' heel by supporting the appointment of his daughter, Indira Gandhi, as president of the party organization. But none of us thought of this as the beginning of a terrible nepotism that, fifteen years later, would lead to the shutdown of democracy in the whole of India.

We had not acquainted ourselves sufficiently with Indian history to know that Nehru himself had been anointed leader of the Indian National Congress by his own father while traveling to a nationalist convention in 1929. At first the young Nehru had apparently blushed at the obscene suggestion, but his father had argued that there was no need for such formalities as an election, and by the time the overnight train reached Lahore, Nehru had stopped resisting.

Because we did not know these things, we did not consider it particularly sinister that now Nehru, as his father before him, had placed this political party—so great that it was said the two largest organizations in the world were the Catholic Church and the Indian National Congress—in the hands of his only child, Indira, who had prevailed upon him to dismiss the Kerala government.

This afternoon in 1959 the huge gathering in the Oval Garden of Bombay was to demonstrate against the first major act of corruption in free

India's public life. Though I was on my way to the meeting for adolescent and sensationalist reasons, even I thought what Nehru and his daughter had done was pretty rum. And when I joined that sea of demonstrators, two hundred thousand strong, I experienced a satisfying sense of oneness. Perhaps it had all been some terrible mistake and this aberration would soon be put to rights.

It was a humid day and the overcast sky seemed to press down on the immense crowd packed into the park. Squeezing past people perspiring heavily in the heavy air, I made my way toward the front of the demonstration. There were thousands of trade unionists holding placards claiming that communism was a legitimate road to social justice. There were newspapermen. There were ordinary citizens who objected to an action that smacked of the imperial fiats of the British Raj. There were people from Kerala, shocked by the attack on their democratic rights, accusing Nehru of dismissing their government because it had recently enacted laws giving land to the landless.

Such was the scale of the demonstration that every policeman in Bombay had been called out in case things got out of control. In the middle of that huge gathering I was suddenly surrounded by a cordon of demonstrators who urged me to leave. I objected strongly. I wanted to be part of the action. The trade unionists around me were courteous but firm. This was not a game, they pointed out. The police had tear gas and were preparing to use it. There would be confusion, demonstrators would fall and perhaps be trampled when the cannisters were fired into that tightly packed crowd. No one wanted to be responsible for harm coming to a lady.

Under the circumstances I had little option but to agree to be escorted from the park by eight men, linking arms to make way for me through the crowd. A few minutes later the firing began.

In the years that followed, there would be other demonstrations when state governments were dismissed, but the police would no longer hold their fire until the women and children had left.

And we would learn through bitter experience how the strain of centralizing power could make the republic creak like an overloaded ship, its cargo of disparities too heavy a weight to keep afloat.

17

Congress Culture

After studying at Cambridge University I returned to Bombay, and during an academic gathering I met a poet who invited me to visit him for tea. The poet was very exact about the directions to his home, since his poverty condemned him to live in the huge slum on the way to Bombay airport inhabited some said by fifty thousand people, some said by a hundred thousand people.

The poet had been born a Hindu belonging to the lowest caste until he had converted to the Buddhist faith, as Dr. Ambedkar had done ten years earlier, watched by half a million untouchables. Now the poet was a Dalit. The word meant "downtrodden." More than that, he was now a Dalit Panther.

His creed was Dr. Ambedkar's famous speech to untouchables who after five years of nonviolent demonstrations had failed to gain entrance to a Hindu temple.

"If you want self-respect," Dr. Ambedkar had said, "change your religion.

"If you want equality, change your religion.

"If you want power, change your religion.

"That religion which forbids humanitarian behavior between men is not a religion but a penalty.

"That religion which regards the recognition of human dignity as a sin is not a religion but a sickness.

"That religion which allows one to touch a foul animal but not a man is not a religion but a madness."

In Bombay the powerful speech had been adopted by educated untouchables who had formed themselves into a militant movement after converting to the Buddhist faith. They called themselves the Dalit Panthers.

I was familiar with the term "panther." During the years I had spent at university in England, the Vietnam War was at its height, demonstrations were a daily affair, and the main body of student opinion had been sympathetic to the cause of the Black Panthers, the black militants in America.

Back in India I discovered Indian university students were also reading the jailed Eldridge Cleaver's book *Soul on Ice* and women regularly paraded the streets in front of the American Embassy in Delhi with placards demanding FREE ANGELA DAVIS.

And now, in 1969, I found myself having tea with a Dalit Panther in a shack constructed from tin sheets, bits of wood, discarded posters, torn sarongs—any protection from the monsoon rain pouring down with such force it had flooded the slum's mud alleys, turning them into running streams in which pieces of construction material were floating disconsolately.

While the poet squatted on the floor and heated water in a pan over a kerosene burner to make tea, I sat on a plank of wood that had been balanced on bricks, surreptitiously examining his home. Everything was in its place. A few garments hung on a rope that extended across the shelter, tied from one pole to another. Above the kerosene burner he had nailed a picture of Dr. Ambedkar into the tin wall.

He unlocked a small trunk, removing a packet of tea and two steel glasses. I peered over his shoulder into the trunk. Books and papers were neatly stacked on one side; cooking utensils and paper packets filled with rice, flour, lentils, on the other.

"They say the British used divide and rule to control India, but the Congress Party has perfected it," the poet said angrily as he brewed the tea. "As for the Congress culture . . ." His rage would not allow him to complete the sentence.

He didn't have to. I knew what he meant. After twenty years of unchallenged power the great Indian National Congress party had grown moribund, its leaders arguing over the spoils of office, its committee warning its members, "Congress personnel is hopelessly divided—factionalism is pervasive—dissensions and mutual vilification create a revulsion of feelings against the Congress among the people."

The poet handed me a glass of tea and spoke of his hatred of what he called the "Congress culture," practiced by politicians who cynically retained power by playing on the fears of the country's minorities—the Muslims, the lower castes, the Buddhists, the Christians.

"Are you thinking of entering politics?" I inquired.

"A poor man like me?" he asked incredulously. "Against the money and muscle of these politicians who rule over us like kings?"

He went to the kerosene stove to heat some more water, and I surreptitiously hitched up my sari to avoid the water running in rivulets across the mud floor.

Turning, the poet saw me. He waved his arms helplessly to indicate the squalor of the slum outside, the water running across the floor inside, the sodden cloth covering the entrance to his shack. Pointing to the picture on his wall, he told me bitterly that he had the national flag tattooed on his buttocks, because the constitution was hardly worth wiping the national arse with.

"Dr. Ambedkar was wrong. Changing a religion means nothing. Elections mean nothing. For people like us power can only come from the barrel of a gun."

18

Nonviolence

In 1978 an Indian magazine asked me to go to the northeastern border state of Assam, home to twenty million people, and write about the largest nonviolent movement India had seen since Mahatma Gandhi had used nonviolence to end the British Raj.

Nonviolence may have expelled the British from India, but our first lesson in freedom was the violence of Partition and in Assam I discovered we have not yet learned our lesson well.

It was dusk when I reached the capital of Assam and drove to the hill temple that is Assam's holiest place of pilgrimage. With its rice fields stretching to Bangladesh on one side, its wooded hills rising to China's borders on the other, Assam is connected to India by only a narrow corridor of land. But the attempt to capture India's attention had mobilized hundreds of thousands of Assamese into a nonviolent movement that had already closed schools, factories, shops, and India's major oil refinery for nearly a year.

Standing on the hillside high above the mighty Brahmaputra River, I tried to understand this movement whose ranks swelled daily with newcomers prepared to defend what tourist brochures called "The Land of the Red River and the Blue Hills."

In the temple courtyard a frangipani tree dropped white blossoms onto the black stones, the slender petals spinning like hexagons against the darkening sky. Below the temple, the setting sun was throwing the islands in the vast sweep of water into red relief. River steamers from the days of the British Empire, still bearing their battered old JARDINE HENDERSON signs, crossed the crimson water of the great river as mist closed over the fishing villages on the distant bank. Inside the temple the priest had begun the evening devotions, chanting a melancholy melody that seemed to evoke Assam's separation from the rest of India.

We had done little to dispel that sense of isolation. In 1962, when the Chinese Army had invaded India through Assam, Prime Minister Nehru had withdrawn our ill-equipped troops from the occupied state with his infamous radio address, "My heart bleeds for the people of Assam."

Then in 1971 the war for the new nation of Bangladesh had pushed waves of war-weary refugees over India's borders into Assam. They were still there, and the Assamese were demonstrating against what they considered a new occupation. But Prime Minister Indira Gandhi had declared the movement the work of foreign agitators and sent in the Indian Army to disband the protesters and open the oil refinery.

So I could sympathize with the angry young engineer who had asked me, "We are fighting another invasion, and Nehru's daughter sends the Army to fire on us! Is she mad? Is it our fault that the millions of foreigners who are overrunning us today don't speak Chinese?"

But as I watched the lanterns swaying on the steamers far below me and the river turning black in the fading light, I wondered how long Assam's movement to expel foreigners would limit itself to foreigners. How long before it turned on other Indians?

The next day as my car approached the oil installation, I could see large painted billboards

warning NO ENTRY. RESTRICTED AREA. NO UNAUTHO-
RISED PERSONNEL. Obeying the ominous signs at
the entrance gates, we stopped. A guard came
out of the guardhouse with a large security
ledger. My driver carefully filled in the required
information: *Time, Number of Visitors.* Under
the heading *Purpose of Visit* he carefully wrote
down "Picketing." I borrowed the ledger, flip-
ping through its pages. On each page the *Purpose of Visit* column repeated its pedantic entry:
"Picketing." "Picketing." "Picketing."

Despite the ledger entries, I was unprepared
for the enormity of the crowds inside the sprawling oil installation. There were people everywhere—on the verandahs, on the grass, on any
piece of ground where there was some shade
from the fierce sun. Banners proclaimed the
cause: WE WILL GIVE OUR BLOOD BUT NOT OUR OIL.
Under a portrait of Mahatma Gandhi were em-
blazoned UPHOLD MY TEACHINGS. UPHOLD THE CONSTI-
TUTION. KILL ME NOT AGAIN BY KILLING THE PEACEFUL
PICKETERS.

Thousands of boys were lying in rows on the
ground, dressed in sarongs for comfort,
equipped with cigarettes, radios, and magazines
for another night of civil disobedience. Facing
them was a long double-story building crowded
with women preparing food. A man with a
megaphone was shouting out instructions to the

newcomers: where to go for water, where to sleep, where the toilets were.

Buses disgorged increasing numbers of pick-eters next to a wall where a line of giggling schoolgirls sat, dangling their feet over a gutter and comparing earrings.

I asked them if they had met with any resistance from their parents when they joined the picket lines.

"Of course. Our parents told us there are too many boys here. Spending the nights like this, our reputations will be destroyed. Afterwards, who will marry us?"

The giggling got louder until I inquired how they felt about the Army being called out to disband the pickets and start the oil pumping again.

"I would be proud to die for the cause," said one girl with absolute conviction. "We have taken the vow of supreme sacrifice."

"We are not afraid of the Army," declared another girl, whose father was a priest at the temple. "How can the Army be violent to us when we ourselves are nonviolent?"

Because India's need for oil is so great, I thought.

Still, a picket official graciously accepted my congratulations on the wonderful organization.

"Though we didn't really organize anything," he told me proudly. "It just happened. Was it Oscar Wilde who said, 'Crisis needs no rehearsal'? Our movement is a spontaneous mass response to a crisis."

"Chaos needs no rehearsal either," I reminded him.

"Why chaos? What can the Army do against such numbers?" He leaned toward me confidentially. "You know, at our first meetings we asked people to give up going to the cinema and smoking cigarettes until there was not a foreigner left on our soil. They didn't agree. Then we asked if they would give up their lives. Everyone shouted yes."

I immediately lit a cigarette. Who was I to argue with the hundreds and thousands of people who agreed it was easier to give up your life than to give up smoking.

And perhaps both living and smoking are easier to give up than anger—the anger of the non-Assamese university lecturer who demanded, "Peaceful? This movement? Ask my wife!"

The wife, serving tea, said, "I have lived all over India, but I never knew I was a Bengali, not an Indian, until I came here. I am watching what is happening and wondering where it will stop. Women I have cuddled in my lap when they were themselves children now let their own children stand outside my gate yelling, 'Bengali dogs! Get out!' "

Her husband added wearily, "I tell my students, once you think you belong only to a particular part of the country, you deprive yourselves of the wealth of the whole country. Unfortunately, the real fuel of this movement is emotionalism. And in these circumstances anything can happen."

Two nights later I gained some idea of what could happen. The vast and generally peaceful movement was nonetheless full of the simple passion and simplistic rhetoric that breed intimidation.

A storm was threatening as I reached a village already a casualty of that rhetoric. Inside a crowded mud hut insects buzzed around a single hurricane lantern while small children, their eyes huge in the lamplight, listened in fearful fascination to their elders. Outside, waves of fireflies made a confusion of the dark as the voices around me intoned a checklist of horror.

"They beat seventeen men to death in the next village because their ancestors came from another part of India."

"We were lucky. We repulsed the first wave of killers with bamboo sticks. Then other wounded villagers came running to us for help. Together, we were enough to frighten the killers away."

"Twenty-eight villages were put to the torch last night. Why?"

Why, indeed? Whatever happened to India's proud pluralism? Whatever happened to non-violence?

19

Good Housekeeping

Nonviolence was India's creed, but by the time I reached Assam, India had fought three wars in ten years and I had witnessed the last.

In 1971, under Indira Gandhi, we had fought a war with Pakistan that had enabled a mutinous East Pakistan to become the independent nation of Bangladesh. I was reporting that war for television, so I was present when the Indian soldiers were greeted by a delirious Bangladeshi population. I saw the brilliant splashes of color as gladioli and canna lilies were pressed into metallic gun barrels instead of bayonets.

In the company of the Indian Jewish general who had written the terms of the cease-fire, I watched a Sikh general take the surrender of the enemy army, and with profound relief I saw that our young soldiers were obeying their Christian commanding officer and showing only respect to the Bangladeshi girls who had been kept by the hated occupying troops as comfort women in their trenches.

Soon the Indian Army would again distinguish itself by safeguarding the honor of women—but this time the women would be Indian.

The year was 1975 and the prevailing situation was called a revolution. In fact, it was a rather domestic affair concerning an election in Gujarat—a state of hardworking farmers and entrepreneurs who were finding the cost of living too high and whose wives had taken to demonstrating.

The movement against prices in Gujarat started peacefully enough. In the birthplace of Mahatma Gandhi, nonviolent expression was second nature, and the revolution consisted largely of housewives in the state capital pouring out of their doorways at sunset, the hour when they should have been lighting lamps in front of family altars prior to preparing the evening meal.

Finding it impossible to make ends meet and feed their families, the housewives waited until the streetlamps came on. Then they beat their metal platters, their *thali*s, with wooden rolling pins to express their dissatisfaction with rising prices.

The practice rapidly spread throughout the state, and within days the national press was calling the ire of the housewives the Thali Revolution. Needing no signal but the setting sun, no provocation but rocketing prices, in every part of the state from its small towns and villages to its diamond centers and ports, the women of Gujarat banged away at their *thalis*— creating such a din that the state echoed with their displeasure.

The noise was not so great it could be heard a thousand miles away in Delhi, but a solid month of this behavior was making Prime Minister Indira Gandhi nervous. And another factor was involved—a politician's nightmare.

A man called Raj Narain was accusing the Prime Minister of rigging her personal election to Parliament. He had contested that seat and claimed Mrs. Gandhi had misused government funds and officials to defeat him. In fact, he had wrapped a green bandana on his head and grown a beard, vowing he would not shave until the Indian courts reversed the Prime Minister's parliamentary election.

At first he had been dismissed as a clown annoying the Prime Minister, who enjoyed the admiration of the nation. Then the Prime Minister's own actions became erratic. She permitted her inexperienced younger son, Sanjay, to acquire a government license to make fifty thousand "people's" cars a year for his Maruti company, a license repeatedly denied other Indian companies familiar with the manufacture of automobiles. Four hundred acres of land were requisitioned on the outskirts of the capital for the factory premises, evicting the inhabitants of three entire villages. Government financial institutions were pressured into giving Maruti unsecured loans as each attempt to produce a car resulted in embarrassing failures. Finally the Reserve Bank of India, the country's central financial institution, intervened, informing state banks that further unsecured loans would undermine the basis of the country's credit policies. Meanwhile, another company owned by Sanjay Gandhi, together with his elder brother, Rajiv, and their respective wives, was discovered to be acting as an agent for government contracts.

In Parliament, critics across the political spectrum were demanding a judicial inquiry into what they variously called "a disgrace to democracy," "corruption and nepotism," "unlimited corruption." When the Prime Minister blocked every attempt at an inquiry, in 1973 the entire opposition walked out of the House to express their displeasure.

So by 1975 Indians were beginning to pay greater attention to the accusations made by the man in the green bandana. Especially the housewives beating away at their *thali*s in the state of Gujarat, where an election was to be held.

Rattled by the man in the bandana's insistence that Indira Gandhi had won her own seat in Parliament dishonestly, the people of Gujarat were determined not to be robbed of the legitimate results of their state poll.

Stay up all night, they exhorted each other as the date for voting approached. Guard the ballot boxes. Throw cordons of women and children around the voting booths so that no one can switch votes under cover of darkness. Oversee the counting.

All this proved too much for the Prime Minister. Describing the Thali Revolution as a CIA plot and then, with her unique gift for paranoia, as a plot by Amnesty International, she sent in the Indian Army to subdue the housewives of Gujarat.

If, as their tribal brethren had done a decade earlier, the housewives of Gujarat had solemnly exposed their backsides to the symbol of Delhi's imperialism, who knows what the outcome might have been. Instead, they continued to come out at dusk and beat their *thali*s with their rolling pins, deafening the embarrassed troops.

These are not housewives, insisted the agitated Prime Minister from Delhi. They are agents provocateurs. Use tear gas, rubber bullets, yes, live rounds, until this threat to the nation's security is terminated.

At her command the officers of the Indian Army ordered their troops to do something that had happened only once before, when nationalists were making illegal salt in defiance of British laws. Then, a British commanding officer had ordered the Royal Garwhal Rifles to fire on the peaceful protesters. The Garwhal Rifles had refused to follow orders.

Now, receiving the Prime Minister of India's directive, once again Indian troops reversed their arms, informing Delhi that the Indian Army did not shoot at Indian citizens.

20

Hereditary Democracy

For the first twenty-five years of modern India's history, our elected representatives generally conducted themselves as servants of the people, concerned for the nation's welfare.

But a crack appeared in India's shiny new democracy when Nehru dismissed an elected state assembly, setting a precedent that his successors would exploit whenever they felt threatened.

As for our claim to nonviolence, under the proud Nehru we fought a war with China, under the meek Shashtri we fought a war with Pakistan. Then Mrs. Gandhi prosecuted a second war with Pakistan, which helped to create the nation of Bangladesh.

Having split the National Congress and

taken its largest faction to a landslide victory with the slogan "Remove Poverty," at the height of her popularity Mrs. Gandhi turned dynastic, fearful of any political challenge.

Ignoring democratic norms, she dismissed state governments at will and elevated unelected family members to positions of power. To ratify her increasingly bizarre behavior, she manipulated undistinguished but obedient politicians into the highest office in the land.

"If she had asked me to clean her latrine, I would have done so," observed one head of state naïvely. "But she asked me to be President of India."

India was changing from a democracy into a court. Soon it would become a police state.

For the next twenty years horrified Indians would watch in disbelief as our politicians forged ever more unholy alliances to keep themselves in power and succeeded only in losing their own lives in bloodbaths of their own creation.

Created from a dream of nonviolence, India would become a land of assassins and armed crackdowns, of bullet-proof screens and police cordons and bombs.

Presiding over an exponential growth of corruption in public life, our leaders would depend on criminals to ensure electoral success, and soon the criminals would themselves enter Parliament.

The rich diversity on which our survival depended would be used against us—caste against caste, religious group against religious group—until hatred became the pattern of our democracy.

And the Indian Army—the third-largest standing army in the world, a volunteer force so proud of its campaign histories—would be ruthlessly used by India's leaders to force trials of strength with the Indian people, making tragedy inevitable.

21

Mass Transit

One summer night in 1975 while the nation slept, the Prime Minister ended democracy in India.

Indira Gandhi declared a State of Emergency "to defend India's unity and integrity."

For goodness' sake! What on earth had threatened Indian integrity? Well, on June 12 the courts had found Indira Gandhi guilty of "using government personnel to further her electoral prospects." She was forbidden from holding any elected office for the next six years. In view of her lofty office, she was given twenty days to appeal to the Supreme Court of India, but she could no longer act as Prime Minister.

"A week is a long time in politics," the British Prime Minister, Harold Wilson, once said.

But twenty whole days? For a leader who could already sense the sharks circling?

The clock was ticking, so on June 16, at three o'clock in the morning, the Delhi police handcuffed her political opponents and carted them off to jail. That same night power was cut off to newspaper printing presses. When the power was turned on again, the censored newspapers printed blank pages with black borders, announcing the death of India's freedom in their obituary columns.

A week later the President of India declared that an imperiled India was now under the Maintenance of Internal Security Act. Indian citizens could no longer question the grounds on which they were detained. Or invoke habeas corpus—the court's right to view a prisoner and establish that he was well, or even alive. The proclamation was followed by midnight raids and mass arrests across the nation—political opponents, dissenting members of Mrs. Gandhi's own party, students, social workers, journalists, teachers, judges, union leaders, and thousands of innocent bystanders. Even a group of astonished hippies.

The writings of Mahatma Gandhi, Nehru, and other Indian patriots on the right to freedom were forbidden; Mahatma Gandhi's own newspaper was closed by government fiat. And with half the nation's elected representatives in jail, the constitution of India was amended four times.

The first amendment prevented any legal challenge to the declaration of the Emergency.

The second amendment nullified retroactively the judgment against Mrs. Gandhi for corrupt practices, and deprived the courts of jurisdiction over any future electoral malpractices by a Prime Minister.

The third amendment gave India's Prime Minister permanent immunity from any civil or criminal proceedings—not only while occupying office but before assuming office and, just to be on the safe side, after leaving office.

The fourth amendment was particularly poignant. Having lost their fundamental rights, Indian citizens were now given a list of fundamental duties.

Neutered of its constitutional power, the Supreme Court overruled Mrs. Gandhi's sentence. Only Justice Khanna, next in line to become the Chief Justice of India, argued that all these constitutional amendments had become meaningless, since depriving a person of life and liberty without the authority of law was to remove the distinction between a lawless society and one governed by law.

As if to prove his argument, the offices of

over two hundred rebellious Delhi lawyers were bulldozed to the ground. The lawyers marched, black-robed, in silent protest on the Supreme Court. They were promptly arrested as arsonists and looters.

But the poor who objected when their homes were bulldozed for beautification of the city were given no reason for their arrests. And they had no redress against a new population-control program in which government employees were given sterilization quotas that had to be filled if employees wanted promotions or even to keep their jobs.

Villagers were rounded up, police cornered the city's poor, people died of botched operations, doctors who objected to the lack of hygiene were jailed. Meanwhile, nationalized television and radio kept up a barrage of propaganda telling the nation we had never had it so good. After all, each sterilized person was being given a transistor radio by the government.

With awesome inevitability, Mrs. Gandhi raised her younger son, Sanjay Gandhi, to become an unelected center of absolute power, second only to herself in the country.

Equally inevitably, having ruthlessly silenced all dissension, the Prime Minister and her son believed that the massive organized crowds were spontaneous displays of a nation's adulation. And across the border Pakistan was going to the polls.

Determined to prove to the world that she was indisputably the voice of India, assured by intelligence reports that victory was a certainty, Mrs. Gandhi suddenly called a snap election to legitimize her actions.

The elections were to take place in a mere six weeks, but most of India's political leaders were still in jail. To prove the election was not a fiction, they were now released—on parole, required to report their movements to their local police, forbidden to travel.

There was every expectation that Mrs. Gandhi would win. The state-owned radio and television companies were pumping out government propaganda. Newspapers were censored. And now the government raised the salaries of millions of its employees—teachers, factory workers, army personnel, bureaucrats—certain that self-interest would guarantee electoral success.

Everyone knew—though they could not speak of it for fear of being overheard and reported to the police—that India's future rode on this election. What Mahatma Gandhi had done in the 1930s with his Salt March had to be done again in the 1970s, a silent protest of gargantuan proportions. And six weeks was all the time the nation had.

I attended a series of rallies in Delhi in those weeks, learned about through word of mouth. At each rally the crowds grew larger, proving the bush telegraph to be as effective a means of communication as electronics when there is something urgent to convey. While Indira Gandhi addressed meetings in the main parks, with all the attendant panoply of state—police cordons, massive platforms, free transport to bring reluctant attendees back and forth—we strained to hear paroled leaders standing on soapboxes with only a megaphone for amplification.

On the road leading into Delhi University I listened to the redoubtable Madame Pandit, with her Chinese collars and blue-rinsed hair, urging us to vote for freedom. Although she was Nehru's sister, she had needed no nepotistic appointments. She had been the first woman president of the General Assembly of the United Nations, and played a distinguished role in the struggle for India's freedom. Now, despite the fact that she was already in her eighties, Madame Pandit had come out of political retirement to hold meetings all over the capital, appalled by the smashing of the Indian democratic process by her own niece.

At one rally Madame Pandit was speaking to us in Hindustani when she noticed the arrival of camera crews. She broke off her speech to inquire who they were. Learning they were European reporters, she proceeded with her impassioned speech on freedom but translated her words into English, German, and French for the television cameras. It was a tour de force performance. Such effortless sophistication—it made you proud to be an Indian.

Then, only days before the momentous general election, a meeting was held at night in the walled city of Old Delhi, inside the great Friday Mosque built by the Moghul Emperors to face the Red Fort, which was the seat of their empire. For five hundred years this particular area of Delhi had been the goal of those who wished to gain power over India. It was here that the victorious British soldiers had built their army barracks on the harem of the last Moghul Emperor, here that the Union Jack was lowered and the Indian flag unfurled when India became a free nation.

The sun had long since set by the time I reached the rally, but crowds were still streaming onto the grounds of the mosque. To discourage attendance, electricity to the entire area had been cut off by the city administration, and for once the brooding vastness of the mosque dwarfed the narrow streets of the old city crowded with veiled women. Many of its residents were Muslim families who still lived in the same sixteenth-century houses, with interior courtyards and latticed stone balconies and narrow stairways, that their ancestors had occupied. For two long years they had endured the excesses of the Emergency—seen respected elders, or young boys not yet pubescent, forcibly sterilized to fulfill government quotas; seen shops crushed into rubble under the bulldozers' inexorable advance.

Now the darkness, lit only by kerosene lanterns and huge torches, added a somberness to the occasion, almost a magnificence, allowing us to see the great mosque as it must have been seen by the Moghuls themselves, its massive lines looming above us undiminished by the neon strips that would ordinarily have illuminated the bazaars and warrens of streets of the old city.

Two- and three-story houses ringed the mosque. Women in billowing burnooses crowded at the dimly lit balconies like the silhouetted audience in some theater, their shapes negated by folds of black cloth.

There was no space on the wide sandstone steps leading up to the platform, where lanterns threw the features of the speakers into grotesque relief as they addressed the crowds spilling into the streets. We could hardly hear the speakers, but we knew from their shapes who they were. The Imam of the mosque, spokesman for Muslim sentiment, shared the platform with the leader of the right-wing Hindus. Sworn enemies from the time of Partition, they shared a blood hatred. Yet together they were exhorting us to exert our democratic rights. There was the greatest snob in India, Madame Pandit, her hair purple in the lamplight, sitting at the feet of the leader of the untouchables. Ignoring the separations of caste, of class, of gods, the speakers shared the crowded platform while we stood there straining to hear them remind us how our ballots could change history.

Suddenly the women weren't up on the balconies anymore. They were among us, their faces exposed, cloth panels thrown resolutely above their heads, breaking the enormity of purdah to rally against the leader whom they held responsible for dishonoring their menfolk, destroying their homes.

A fortnight later the counting had ended and the government was preparing its victory celebrations.

At two o'clock in the morning I waited with thousands of other Indians in front of the offices of the *Indian Express*. We were milling in the street at that ungodly hour because the newspaper's correspondents were telephoning in the election results from all over the nation, results that the shocked government television and radio stations were not announcing.

Every few minutes a journalist came out of the offices, handed a piece of paper to a thin clerk in gray trousers scribbling with chalk onto a blackboard, raced back inside again. While we held our breath, the clerk scribbled the latest election results onto the spotlighted blackboard. Each time a candidate of Mrs. Gandhi's party lost a seat, money was flung at him for bringing good news and he blinked at us in surprise through the currency floating like confetti over his head.

When Mrs. Gandhi lost her own seat in Parliament by a massive margin, women began flinging their jewelry at the clerk.

In all the cheering I heard someone say, "She got what she deserved. Why did she trouble the poor?"

22

Losing It

The Emergency was India's watershed, compromising the President and Supreme Court, who rubber-stamped it; the bureaucrats and police, who enforced it; the national radio and television, who lauded it, unchallenged by a gagged press.

Determined that Indians should understand the process by which their liberty could so easily be stolen, India's new Prime Minister, Morarji Desai, held a public inquiry into the causes of the Emergency, and the hearings were broadcast on national television. While Parliament reversed Mrs. Gandhi's constitutional amendments, day after day hundreds of people appeared before the Shah Commission to describe their experiences—which too often included torture. Their evidence was then published in the *Shah Commission Report*, providing a unique examination of India's democracy.

One thing the hearings proved conclusively: we desperately needed political alternatives to control the excesses of the party that had ruled India these thirty years. But our first alternative, the Janata Party, was formed under the most unpropitious circumstances—its leaders on parole, unable to meet and resolve their conflicting agendas. In power, those leaders were soon imitating the behavior of their Congress predecessors.

As the Janata Party disintegrated, Indira Gandhi toured the nation, denying responsibility for the excesses of the Emergency and offering a "Government That Works." At the next election, having no political alternative, the nation voted Mrs. Gandhi back to power. Copies of the *Shah Commission Report* on the Emergency were immediately seized and destroyed.

Now the scramble for power was on in earnest. While we spent the next decades looking for that elusive prize of a genuinely multiparty system, our leaders looked for more ways to divide us.

But at least we knew that the categorical verdict against the Emergency had safeguarded our democracy forever.

Alas, we had not thought to defend ourselves against the politics of religion. We were so certain no Indian politician would dare use religion to gain power. Not after the horrors of Partition. Everyone knew religion was India's line of no return. Beyond that line lay chaos.

But a social reformer called the Conscience of the Nation knew India better than we did. Minutes after the Emergency was declared, the terminally ill Jayaprakash Narayan was pulled from his bed and taken off to jail, the first casualty of India's lost liberty. Turning to his jailers, he explained Mrs. Gandhi's behavior by reciting the famous Sanskrit lines that describe the madness of Sita, the god Rama's wife.

In Indian mythology Sita and her brother-in-law, Laxman, are wandering the jungle, waiting for Rama to find them. Before Laxman goes to hunt for food, he draws three lines in the dust, warning Sita if she steps over them he can no longer protect her; but through the trees, Sita sees a golden deer that calls to her in Rama's voice, and she steps over the line of protection into chaos.

That night when embarrassed jailers put handcuffs on a leader who had walked at Mahatma Gandhi's side during the movement for India's freedom, Jayaprakash Narayan recited:

> *"No one sees a golden deer,*
> *No one hears a golden deer,*
> *Until the times are bad and the mind is*
> *   disordered."*

Now the times were again bad.

We were being told that our rich pluralism, the diversity which defined us, was a sickness, an alien concept of Western secularism grafted onto India.

We were about to face our second watershed.

India's leaders had seen the golden deer of power running through India's trees and it was calling to them in God's voice.

23

God's Work

When Britain's expatriate Sikhs celebrated the three hundredth anniversary of their faith, in the Royal Albert Hall in London, they invited the Indian writer Khushwant Singh to speak on the occasion. Singh had once been a member of the Indian diplomatic mission in London. His novel *Train to Pakistan* was considered a classic on the horrors of Partition. And he was a Sikh.

Unfazed by the red velvet chairs and royal boxes of the Albert Hall, Singh rose to his feet and shouted lustily to the packed chamber, "Beloved ones, do you remember the taste of unleavened bread?"

There was a roar of response from the turbanned audience, hearing the earthy language of the Punjab farmers. Back in India, their industrious relatives were turning Punjab into the granary of India, those relatives who were not in the Indian Armed Forces mostly as frontline troops.

"And do you remember the taste of black lentils?" Whistles and stamping shook the chamber in nostalgia for the diet to which the audience ascribed their robust strength.

"And what about the taste of mustard spinach and sugarcane juice?"

Cheering Sikhs were on their feet, shouting their battle cry, "Victory to the guru's faithful! Victory to his men of truth!"

It was a common response to anything that moved them. The Sikhs are a people proud of their martial history, which is why they still wear their long hair under a turban—the sign by which Sikhs once identified each other on the battlefield defending their religion. In fact, during the religious persecution of the fanatical Moghul Emperor Aurangzeb, even Hindu families often gave one son to the Sikh faith, to keep their line alive.

Yet in their holiest shrine, the Golden Temple of Amritsar, symbolic of the spiritual power of God, with its library containing books collected over five centuries and manuscripts written by the gurus of their faith, serenity is sacrosanct.

It was, that is, until Mrs. Gandhi and her

younger son supported an obscure Sikh priest named Bhindranwale to bring down the state government of Punjab.

Armed with automatic rifles, confident of the central government's protection, the priest and his followers entered the Golden Temple. From its safety the priest declared that anyone not a Sikh should be evicted from Punjab. While he issued fanatical edicts, his followers beat up those Sikhs who dared to raise their voices in protest, shot dead the Sikh Inspector General of Police, and intimidated non-Sikhs into fleeing. Soon Punjab was an armed camp. Inside the state Hindus were being terrorized; outside the state Sikhs were being terrorized. For the first time in India's history, there was hatred between Hindu and Sikh.

On the grounds of restoring stability, Mrs. Gandhi assumed control of Punjab. But the monster she had created so unthinkingly could no longer be controlled. The priest was now so powerful he was being courted by other political parties. He was now so powerful he didn't want to be courted—he wanted his own country. Having run out of options, she dispatched the Indian Army to oust the priest and in the pitched battle the great library of the Sikhs was destroyed, innocent worshippers were killed by cross fire. Blood had at last stained the white marble floor of the Golden Temple.

To avenge those deaths, Mrs. Gandhi was herself shot by a Sikh bodyguard even as she was campaigning for a new general election. Squads of thugs responded by murdering thousands of Sikhs in Delhi.

Sikh temples were set alight, priests guarding holy books were torched. Anyone who wore a turban was attacked. To save their lives, the vastly outnumbered Sikhs cut their hair, but they were butchered anyway. The Indian Army, which could have prevented the killings, was confined to barracks by a government now under her elder son Rajiv Gandhi's control, while the only Indian general who had ever taken the surrender of an enemy army was called a traitor because he was a Sikh, his wife and children forced to flee their home to seek sanctuary with shocked strangers.

I accompanied a Sikh woman to the Delhi suburb of Trilokpuri, which had seen some of the worst carnage. Mistaking me for a member of the dead Prime Minister's family, people sidled up to me and proudly boasted how many defenseless Sikh families they had killed in their homes.

"How did you know where they lived?"

"We were given lists with their addresses. And cans of kerosene."

"By whom?"

"You know. Everybody knows."

They could not understand my rage. They certainly would not have understood the rage of the Indians flooding into a privately run relief camp with food and clothing for the wounded women and children who had survived the killings, where priests of every faith were trying to comfort the bereaved families, people of every religion trying to alleviate their anguish. All around me I heard the incandescent fury of ordinary Indians that the ruling party had kept the Army in barracks, claiming the massacre was a spontaneous outpouring of enraged grief. If this was true, they asked, why were so few Sikhs attacked in states not governed by Mrs. Gandhi's party? Later they would ask why Rajiv Gandhi as Prime Minister would not hold an inquiry into the slayings, despite the detailed case histories assembled by a citizens' committee headed by a Chief Justice.

Still, with Mrs. Gandhi's assassination and the civil war in Punjab, it seemed no leader would, in the sinister understatement used in India, "play the religious card" again.

We had forgotten Kashmir.

Nestled below the holy Himalayas, Kashmir

possessed a unique religious mysticism. Kashmir's Islam was inspired by the ecstatic visions of the Sufi poet-saints; her Hinduism was a product of the great sage Shankaracharya, who had urged pilgrims to travel India from the beaches on the Indian Ocean to her highest mountain caves and learn that they belonged to a common world. Indeed, during the carnage of Partition Mahatma Gandhi had described peaceful Kashmir as "an island of sanity."

But shortly before her death Indira Gandhi had dismissed Kashmir's democratically elected government and installed a puppet government. Three years later Rajiv Gandhi did the same, and the beautiful Kashmir Valley erupted in violence, convinced it would never get justice from an imperialist Delhi. Demagogic priests played upon the insecurities of a largely Muslim population, and Kashmir's mysticism was replaced by fanaticism. Those who did not believe in Islam were terrorized out of the valley. The Army was sent in. Soon a hundred thousand Hindu refugees were eking out a miserable existence in camps waiting to return to their homes; twenty thousand Muslims could never return, killed in police and army action.

As if the deadly adventurism in Punjab and Kashmir were not enough, we soon learned that Indira Gandhi had been financing and training

Sri Lanka's Tamil insurgents in order to gain the support of India's thirty million Tamil voters, angry over injustices to the Sri Lankan Tamils.

Under Rajiv Gandhi, that training intensified. Sri Lankan guerrilla leaders were received in Delhi as guests of the Indian government. India violated Sri Lankan airspace to drop supplies to beleaguered Tamils. Finally, an intimidated Sri Lanka invited India to dismantle the insurrection, but when our army reached Sri Lanka, it discovered the rebels it had trained didn't want to be dismantled.

During the next three years fifteen hundred Indian soldiers would be killed by Tamil guerrillas before a new Prime Minister, V. P. Singh, finally brought our demoralized troops home, leaving behind a festering Tamil hatred of India's leaders.

Punjab, Kashmir, Tamil guerrillas—so much damage unleashed in five short years. And the worst was yet to come.

Years ago, while conducting the negotiations for partitioning the subcontinent, Lord Wavell, Viceroy of India, had observed, "The more I see of these Indian politicians, the more I despair of India."

Now Indians would despair of their politicians as the genie of Hindu-Muslim hatred was once again released into mainstream Indian politics.

In 1985 the Supreme Court of India granted an illiterate Muslim woman maintenance payments for herself and her children from the husband who had divorced her. The landmark judgment applied to all Indian women. But in 1986, to win the support of fundamentalist Muslim voters, Rajiv Gandhi used his brute majority in Parliament to pass a new law. Henceforth, Muslim women would be subject to medieval interpretations of the shariat, Islamic religious law on marriage and divorce.

Moderate Muslim opinion and the vast majority of Indians were appalled. If the votes of Muslim fundamentalists were to be bought in this fashion, what would fundamentalist Hindus demand? Had the Prime Minister forgotten that the Hindu Laws of Manu sanctioned untouchability? Couldn't he see that naked opportunism was setting the cause of equality before the law back by centuries in India? Where would this end?

That question was answered within weeks in the small northern temple town of Ayodhya.

Many Hindus believe Ayodhya to be the birthplace of the god-king Rama, and it is ringed with temples claiming to be the site of the god-king's birth. Among the temples is a single sixteenth-century mosque identified by some Hindu fundamentalists as the actual site of Rama's birth. To prevent religious disputes, the mosque had been padlocked for half a century. Now, angered Hindu fundamentalists prevailed upon a district judge to open the monument for worship by Hindus.

Suddenly remembering that Indian Hindus outnumbered Indian Muslims by six to one, Rajiv Gandhi permitted the fundamentalists to lay a foundation stone for a temple in the disputed precincts. Then he arrived at the mosque to launch his campaign for a new general election, promising to give India "Ram Rajya," the government of the god-king Rama.

Only a Marxist had the courage to observe dryly that India needed latrines more than India needed temples or mosques. The wise observation was ignored. Seizing the political weapon that had so carelessly been placed in its hands, the Hindu nationalist party, the Bharatiya Janata Party (BJP), claimed to be the only party able to give India the government of Rama. Still, Rajiv Gandhi lost the general election, the Hindu nationalists didn't win it either, and India gained a brief respite when a new government threw a police cordon around the town and jailed religious rabble-rousers.

But the barred Hindu fanatics kept the issue

of the temple simmering, their rhetoric becoming increasingly violent as a new general election approached. And the BJP grew steadily more powerful as it made the temple the central plank of its election campaign. Vowing to destroy the mosque and build a great Hindu temple on its ruins, BJP leaders toured the subcontinent exhorting every Hindu village in India to fire a brick for the new Rama temple.

Campaigning for the next election, Rajiv Gandhi was blown up by a Tamil woman guerrilla wired as a human bomb.

India's new Prime Minister, heading a minority government, did not want to alienate the Hindu nationalists. The BJP was now the second-largest party in Parliament.

Reassured by Prime Minister Rao's inactivity, one December morning in 1992 a mob of three hundred thousand Hindu fanatics, in the presence of BJP leaders, demolished the Ayodhya mosque with their bare hands, planting images of Rama in the rubble.

Massive Hindu-Muslim riots followed. Twelve hundred kilometers from the mosque armed gangs claiming to be the Shiv Sena, the BJP's closest political allies, began massacring Muslims across the length and breadth of Maharashtra state, insisting they were Pakistani spies. For a week the state capital, Bombay, the engine of India's economy, shut down in fear. Within a month Bombay would shut down again as ten bombs exploded simultaneously across the city, damaging luxury hotels, corporate offices, the century-old Stock Exchange, killing and injuring hundreds.

How could this happen? Only fifteen years earlier, during the Emergency, I had seen the BJP leaders standing shoulder to shoulder with Muslim priests on the steps of India's largest mosque, urging us to bring democracy back to the nation.

"Why are you engaged in this insanity?" I asked one of those leaders now.

"We are just doing what the Congress Party does," she replied. "But we are doing it better."

Very much better. They had drawn up a list of other mosques that had to be destroyed. Indeed, one of their followers had written a whole book to prove that another Muslim monument had been built over a Hindu place of worship. His claim had even caught the attention of the *New York Times*, and his supporters were clamoring to be heard.

The Taj Mahal, they said, was an affront to the Hindu faith. It must also be pulled down.

24

Stamping

During an election in the eighties a young woman, Nalini Singh, happened to be at a polling booth when the voting was suddenly disrupted by armed men. Brandishing their weapons to disperse the frightened voters, the men stamped all the ballot papers and, at gun point, forced the election official to seal the ballot boxes. The young woman was so appalled by what she had seen, she decided to make a television film so that the whole of India could watch their electoral system being hijacked.

In her film the director interviewed the gangs hired by political parties of every persuasion to make sure their candidates won. Masking their faces to hide their identities, the gangsters told the interviewer how they provided what they proudly referred to as the "muscle power" of Indian politics.

First they bribed the villagers. If that didn't work, they slapped the village elders around. If beating up respected members of the community didn't work, then limbs were broken—an arm here, a leg there. If that didn't work, a gang member said with mock ruefulness that the odd voter had to be shot. But if the villagers or the factory workers or the slum dwellers still insisted on exercising their franchise, then there was always the bomb, which made a big impression on the confidence of the voters.

To guarantee a sweeping majority for their boss, the gang members also captured whole polling booths and stamped every ballot with their candidate's symbol—in the manner that had moved the director to make the film in the first place. When she asked the gang members if they were not afraid of the law, they laughed.

The police, the bureaucrats, the judges—all were hired by the state. And their candidate would be in control of state power. Who would dare to punish them?

Of course, many gang leaders have found it convenient to enter politics personally. With their "muscle power" they can guarantee victory and keep the spoils of the system for themselves.

25

The Greatest Show
on Earth

After the heady euphoria of seeing the communist bloc countries throw off the shackles of the Soviet Empire, the world is discovering that the combination of political freedom and economic scarcity is a lot more dangerous than any number of Molotov cocktails. Commentators wring their hands as they contemplate the potentially explosive situation in Eastern Europe, where all those longed-for freedoms are facing all those empty stores.

But for fifty years in India those dangerous freedoms have been maintained by millions of people with empty bellies who know each election is a poker game being played for the highest stakes—their future.

So there was great interest in the country in

1989 when the Republic of India went to the polls for its ninth general election. The suddenness of the announcement and the speed with which the election was to take place—the bare minimum of time allowed by the Indian constitution—were calculated to ensure that the ruling government would be returned to power. And, believing the young to be partial to himself, Prime Minister Rajiv Gandhi had recently lowered the voting age from twenty-one to eighteen. As a result, in this election half a billion voters were to exercise their franchise.

Five hundred million voters. Visualize every voter in the United States and Canada added to every voter in Eastern Europe and Western Europe—voting simultaneously in all their different languages to determine a common government. Then think of the physical enormities of putting such a huge electoral machine into operation.

Three weeks before an election, candidates must file their nomination papers and receive their political symbols. Symbols are a necessity in India—where half the electorate can neither read nor write, and votes by recognizing a picture. Often a political party will put up an outsider with no chance of winning just so his symbol will be confused with the symbol of a powerful opponent by people unaccustomed to looking at small images in print on a piece of paper.

Once the nominations have been filed, only twenty-one days remain before voting. Now the Election Commission must print the ballots. A seemingly easy task? Not in India. The Election Commission must get the names and symbols of all the candidates correct on half a billion ballot papers—in seventeen different languages, each with individual scripts. Then the ballot papers must be conveyed to the vast number of polling booths across the nation, one booth for every thousand voters—from the inaccessible mountains of Ladakh on the very borders of Tibet to the farthest desert areas of Rajasthan on the borders of Pakistan to the southern coasts of Kerala on the edge of the Indian Ocean.

As political consciousness grows, so does the number of candidates, and in this 1989 election a bemused television announcer showed a ballot paper from a single constituency that had the names of one hundred twenty-two different candidates printed next to their one hundred twenty-two pictorial symbols. The actual ballot paper was the size of a newspaper page, and the announcer demonstrated that it took more than three minutes to fold the ballot and insert it inside a box.

While the Election Commission is dealing

with these logistical nightmares, the campaigning begins in earnest. And campaigning in an Indian general election is political theater of the craziest dimensions.

Songs. Street plays. Video films. Poets introducing candidates with specially composed odes. Campaign vehicles turned with mad invention into motorized chariots inspired by mythology. Personal appearances by miracle workers and godmen, film stars and priests. Bazaar jingles satirizing the claims of the contestants. Massive political meetings attended by half a million people, door-to-door canvassing for individual votes.

The sheer force of the Indian electoral process has introduced a new word into the dictionary of democracy—Wave—to describe such a furious display of voter preference that it sweeps all calculation before it.

But to skeptics the word "Wave" suggests an electorate that can be duped. As Malcolm Muggeridge said, a man who can barely feed himself is not a man who can be politically conscious. So those millions of illiterate and starving voters who produce a wave must in fact constitute a mob, capable of being manipulated through populist propaganda or intimidated through the use of force.

To examine populism first. In the fifties market penetration was thought to be the best way of getting a message to the Indian people. At that time the Coca-Cola Company led the field, and our government invited Coca-Cola to distribute contraceptives along with their soft drinks. But villagers who needed to walk twenty miles to reach drinking water were hardly in a position to buy the paradise promised with the purchase of fizzy drinks, and the project was aborted. Once again government radio became the instrument of preaching population control.

By the seventies television had made its entrance into the Indian political arena. Like the radio, Indian television—this mighty weapon of communication—was controlled by government. But for the first time both were now used for political ends.

In 1975 Indira Gandhi declared a State of Emergency and embarked on a program of mass sterilization of the male population. To compensate the sterilized individuals for their pain, their outraged dignity, and their frequent sepsis, they were each given a transistor radio. On television and over those cynically given transistor radios, the Indian masses were bombarded with a propaganda barrage telling them how wonderful things were under the benevolent reign of Mrs. Gandhi and her family.

Knowing every voice of dissent had been silenced, this illiterate and frightened mob turned their radio dials to the BBC World Service. As a result, they were better informed than their government. And when the government finally called a general election in 1977, these same illiterate voters threw it out of power with a massive wave.

But they had not elected an effective government. India's first experiment with a non-Congress government crumbled and the voters turned once again to Indira Gandhi. Unsure of the electorate's loyalty, practicing a politics fought with its back to the wall, she undermined the elected government of Punjab, and that ill-advised action eventually cost Mrs. Gandhi her life.

Still, Rajiv Gandhi looked like the beginning of a new politics. A pleasant young man who smiled a lot and showed great interest in computer technology, he promised to cleanse Indian politics of corruption and take the nation into the twenty-first century. He even acquired the sobriquet of India's Mr. Clean. Riding a wave of sympathy after his mother's assassination, in 1984 Rajiv Gandhi won the most massive electoral mandate in Indian history.

Now India had at its disposal electronic communications. A country that sorely lacked drinking water was given satellite dishes to link a medieval culture to an electronic marketplace, and the staggering power of this new form of market penetration was used to market a single product—Rajiv Gandhi and the virtues of his government.

In living color, we were entering the age of disco democracy. Think of the following panaceas offered to a country with India's problems by her Prime Minister in the years leading up to the elections.

American Presidents jog. So the Prime Minister of India instructs his cabinet to get into jogging suits. Comprised mostly of fat middle-aged party bosses, the Indian cabinet is no ideal of physical beauty. But at least their traditional garments, evolved over centuries to accentuate the positive, disguise their more unaesthetic contours. Now they are required to put on gray jogging suits, and led by their Prime Minister to the theme song from *Chariots of Fire* blaring over loudspeakers wired to lampposts, they unhappily run around the main streets of the capital—their exertions beamed by television across the nation.

An astonished India asks, Why are the men who control our destiny dressed in this peculiar way? And what are they running from?

Earlier the nation watched an even more bizarre event. Rajiv Gandhi decided to reenact

Mahatma Gandhi's famous Salt March—though it was more a Salt Stroll, as it lasted only for the short duration of the photo opportunities necessary for television. And far from being nonviolent, it bristled with a special security force raised by the Prime Minister himself—Black Cat commandos in black leather boots and black fatigues and chic black berets and submachine guns, followed by convoys of security men and political groupies shouting slogans in praise of their leader, whose government was still taxing salt the way the British Empire had done.

Here was proof of an entire government's faith in McLuhan's claim—the medium is the message. After all, half the Indian electorate could not read or write. Half the Indian electorate was unable to earn one meal a day. How could it distinguish between the medium in which information was conveyed and the accuracy of the information being conveyed?

But television spectaculars were not enough to preserve the massive mandate Rajiv Gandhi had received only five years before. India's Mr. Clean was seen as presiding over a politics of corruption unprecedented in a nation that thought it had witnessed every form of venality. There was even widespread belief that Rajiv Gandhi and his wife had robbed the Indian exchequer of millions in defense kickbacks during the purchase of the Swedish-made Bofors gun. His own Defense Minister, V. P. Singh, resigned in disgust to lead the fight against Gandhi's government.

Now Mahatma Gandhi's pacifist grandson entered politics to contest Rajiv Gandhi's seat. Though sharing a name, they were in no way related, as the pacifist Rajmohan Gandhi discovered in a baptism of fire from Prime Minister Gandhi's organizers—his workers beaten up, his election agent taking six bullets in the stomach, his voters' polling booths captured. But then, the pacifist hadn't understood that India was up for grabs.

There appeared to be no overriding issue which defined this election. No Emergency to end. No warring coalition to be dismissed. No sympathy to be expressed. As for corruption, India had grown weary witnessing the cupidity of her leaders. So in this, India's ninth general election, political personalities, journalists, pollsters, tea shop pundits were all asking the same question. Would there be another wave?

But the voter was keeping his cards close to his chest until election day. Well, not every voter. Some voters put up posters saying WANTED! MEMBER OF PARLIAMENT! MISSING FOR FIVE YEARS.

Others were even more explicit. A cabinet

minister was canvassing his constituency, surrounded for reasons of status by gun-toting security police and televisions crews. Aware of the cameras on him, the minister stopped at a village and graciously invited a young man through the security cordon. The young man—a poor farmer—waited politely as the minister recited a string of election promises.

"And so I ask for your help," the minister ended with an assured smile. "Vote for me."

"Five years ago I voted for you," the young farmer replied, smiling shyly. "But you were very busy and could not return from Delhi to look into our problems. So I borrowed money to buy a railway ticket and traveled hundreds of miles to see you. When I got to your house, I told your guards I would wait as long as necessary to meet you. You were my Member of Parliament. You had promised I could come to you for help. After many hours you finally sent me a message. You did not want to see me. And your guards were to slap me for daring to disturb you. Now you have come to me, asking for my help. And I am giving you the same answer."

In full view of the Indian press, the young man slapped the minister across the face, daring—if only for a brief Sisyphean moment—to demand accountability before security guards descended on him.

"The sheer might of India's democracy stirs the blood," the *Economist* magazine wrote when the election results were declared. "The average Indian earns less than $25 a month and likelier than not is unable to read. This did not stop the country's half a billion voters from standing up squarely to their political masters—who between elections lord it over them and often steal from them—uttering one defiant NO after another."

And what a NO this was. With the single exception of Bengal's, every governing party—state and national—was swept out of power. And the Indian voter provided a resounding answer to the excesses of a brute majority by giving no party a majority.

In his first address to the newly elected Parliament, the new Indian Prime Minister, V. P. Singh, acknowledged, "The people of India have forced us to recognize the heterogeneous nature of our country. In creating a situation where political parties must depend on each other for support and govern by consensus, the Indian voter has demanded that politics in India change from the politics of personality to the politics of issue."

The Indian voter got his wish. At the next general election the issue would be class war. The one after it would be fought on the issue of religion. Each time the electorate would deny political power not just to those who claimed the mantle of inherited power, but to a new breed of political demagogues.

In fact, for ten years the voter would refuse any political party a majority. But while the voter was displaying his displeasure with those in power, the inattentive Indian politician was acquiring the assets of power and indulging in the politics of real estate.

Especially in Delhi—where politicians routinely demand palatial government properties as their due for having once held public office and where even the city center has been renamed, although the city's planning instructions expressly state, "The names of existing streets should not be changed. The renaming of streets not only creates confusion for post offices and the public but also deprives people of a sense of history."

On the other hand, renaming streets has the advantage of allowing politicians to rewrite history. So, government residences are requisitioned for family memorials; monuments, airports, parks, are renamed; public money is channeled into private family trusts; national institutions are used to provide lifetime sinecures for politicians' relatives. Rajiv Gandhi even ingeniously made the budget of India into a family memorial: subsidies to agriculture are now always attributed to Nehru, welfare schemes for the poorest sectors of society to Indira Gandhi, youth employment and educational projects to Rajiv Gandhi—converting the citizen's own money into the politician's gift.

Seeing our highest leadership set the fashion, cities all over the country are now littered with familiar places bearing unfamiliar names belonging to politicians yearning for immortality.

But while our politicians protect themselves against their own impermanence with their self-serving memorials, the country's permanence depends on the continued existence of the Indian Parliament, designed by its British architect as a circle to contain all of India's warring aspirations within its embrace. India has already faced two threats that should have destroyed that Parliament more effectively than any bomb placed under its foundations—political totalitarianism, when all democratic process was suspended; and civil war, when religious sectarianism was unleashed.

Yet in Punjab at the very height of the troubles, when they were being urged by their political and religious leaders to kill each other, Hindu and Sikh farmers did not do so. Their restraint made it possible for Punjab to have peace again.

And a High Court judge, a man whose position and salary depended on government, had the courage to confront the most powerful person in India and find Prime Minister Indira Gandhi guilty of electoral corruption. During the trial, when every imaginable pressure was being brought to bear on him—from money to intimidation—Justice Sinha repeatedly told the Prime Minister not to perjure herself, and informed a courtroom crowded with sycophants and security personnel that they were not to jump to their feet when the Prime Minister entered the witness box.

"In this courtroom," he noted severely, "you may only rise for the law."

In the years since Justice Sinha's judgment, the combined pressure exerted by Indian society has slowly changed Indian politics, and the results are beginning to show.

Today the Supreme Court is sentencing leaders across the political spectrum on corruption charges—Prime Ministers, members of the cabinet, leaders of all the largest political parties.

Today the Election Commission has finally banned the passing of populist bills on the eve of an election, and government media can no longer be used for political propaganda.

Today India's two hundred million lower

castes have their own political party and are impressively represented in other political parties.

Today the authorities are enforcing a fundamental principle enshrined in our constitution—that the rhetoric of religious hatred is an illegal use of the political process.

Ironically, there is no problem that has arisen in other democracies—many of them older and richer than India—which India has not struggled to surmount. Sectarianism. Affirmative action. Political assassination. Civil war. Unstable coalitions. The electronic marketing of political aspirants. Separatism. Corruption.

The wonder is that India still exists to surmount them. Not only Indians think so. Commenting on the general election of 1996, an editorial in the *Financial Times* of London noted, "The democracy of India is a wonder of the world."

And its guardian is not the politician so beloved of feature writers but the faceless, nameless, all-enduring Indian voter.

PART FOUR

26

Getting There

As the pace of India's exchanges with the outside world accelerates, there is a growing demand both inside the country and abroad for some comprehensible definition of what India actually is. Definitions are hard to come by, but there are some great descriptions.

When Mark Twain visited India at the end of the nineteenth century, he wrote of the delirium he hoped would never leave him when he saw

the land of dreams and romance, of fabulous wealth and fabulous poverty, of splendor and rags, of palaces and hovels, of famine and pestilence, of genii and giants and Aladdin lamps, of tigers and elephants, the cobra and the jungle, the country of a hundred nations and a hundred tongues, of a thousand religions and two million gods, cradle of the human race, birthplace of human speech, mother of history, grandmother of legend, great-grandmother of tradition, whose yesterdays bear date with the moldering antiquities of the rest of the nations—the sole country under the sun that is endowed with imperishable interest for alien prince and alien peasant, for lettered and ignorant, wise and fool, rich and poor, bond and free, the one land *all* men desire to see, and having seen once, by even a glimpse, would not give that glimpse for the shows of all the rest of the globe combined.

More modestly, India has traditionally described herself as Karma Bhoomi, the Land of Experience, where everything has happened so often before that even history is reduced to troublesome echoes in an empty cave. But no experience in the Land of Experience, nothing in all her yesterdays, has equipped her for a world where her faith in the encompassing unity of life is in daily, even hourly collision with the explosion of fragmented information coming from outside.

Dismissing the possibility of ever defining India, in 1945 the writer Alex Aronson noted ascerbically that India was a civilization, and "civilization is always a process: not a being but a becoming."

Half a century later that observation still proves astute. Somehow India has managed to stay a civilization, still unpredictable, still surprising, still defying definition. Maybe India's indolence preserves her. Or her traditional fascination with unifying what appears fragmented. In any case, in a world of perpetual motion India remains a perpetual becoming, a vast and protean sea of human improvisation on the great dance of time.

27

Reading

"Sahib! Latest from Plato, *The Republic*! Also, James Hadley Chase. P. G. Wodehouse. You want *Catcher in the Rye*, sahib? *Mad* magazine? But sahib, just now unpacked. At least sample *Little Dorrit* by Charles Dickens."

Learning to read in India meant hearing its pleasures shouted at you by pavement booksellers before you even knew how to read. It meant watching the animation on the faces of grown-ups bending over volumes displayed on threadbare scraps of carpet while the booksellers slapped another two books together to loosen the dust kicked up by passing pedestrians, cyclists, cars before whispering conspiratorially, "*Anna Karenina*, sahib. *Madame Bovary*. Hot books, sahib, only this minute arrived. Believe it or not, tomorrow no copies remaining."

Surely there was no other country in the world where booksellers jumped onto the steps of moving trains, clinging with one hand to the iron bars of a window and with the other pushing forward a cane basket brimming with books—cajoling, exhorting, begging you to read. Or where the ability to read was thought synonymous with a longing to read.

In a country where illiteracy is so widespread, the capacity to read is treated with a respect bordering on awe, and maidservants who could neither read nor write made sure we steered our way past the alphabet into those boring primers that described English schoolchildren named Jane and John endlessly running or jumping. Their glee in our achievements increased as our reading improved and we were able to repay the stories we had learned while sitting in their laps—tales of gods and warrior kings and manipulative ascetics who had cheated their way into immortality—with stories from our books of sleeping beauties and frog princes and the extraordinary adventures of Tom Thumb. Because of them the world of the imagination was opened to us, becoming as tangible as the corporeal world, as tangible as the next book waiting to be read by flashlight under the covers when they sent us to bed. And the act of reading became a pleasure so intense that adults often treated it as a vice when they could not draw us from our books to eat or bathe.

However contradictory adults were about our reading habits, they were consistent in demanding respect for the book itself. To deface a book was unthinkable. To put your feet on a book—container of knowledge and thought—was considered an act of such grossness it provoked the contempt of the entire household.

Reading was for us a significant part of the comfort of childhood, indeed a necessary comfort when we were sent off as infants to boarding schools while our parents struggled for India's independence. In darkened dormitories with the monsoon rain beating so heavily on the tin roofs it almost drowned our sobs of homesickness, we could be tricked from our loneliness by the teacher's voice reading tales of Harry the Horse and citizens who played games of chance; or the fortunes of Mrs. Bennett's daughters; or mehitabel signing off to her cockroach with the inspiring sentiment "toujours gai archy toujours gai."

When we got home from school, there were always more books waiting as gifts. Bought by others, not chosen ourselves, these books carried an aura of duty. Fortunately, relatives paying morning calls on our parents would sometimes circle our heads with crisp rupee notes to remove the evil eye, pressing the money between our fingers. Now with cash in hand we were in a position to buy our own books, and the purchase of two books could enable you to read a hundred, thanks to the lending library.

But these were not the lending libraries of the First World. These were secret, shifting Indian libraries that fit into garishly painted tin trunks small enough to be strapped onto the backs of bicycles ridden by librarians who were usually clerks moonlighting from government offices. And their locations were learned about only through word of mouth.

Our favorite library took up three rungs on the wrought-iron fire escape behind O. N. Mukherjee's Emporium in Calcutta. My aficionado elder brother assured me it contained the finest collection of Westerns in the whole world. By investing a fraction of a rupee and including some of your own books in the corpus of the library, you could borrow as many Louis L'Amours and Zane Greys as you could stomach. Or two-in-ones by lesser known writers featuring a picture of an Apache on one cover and, when you turned the book around and upside down, a picture of a mounted cowboy with blazing six-guns on the other. Sometimes, thanks to the librarian's definition of a Western, you might find a Jack London or a Stephen Crane and by this happy mistake be drawn into the worlds of other writers of action—Joseph Conrad, Alexandre Dumas, Leo Tolstoy.

Or opposite the Chinese shoemaker there would appear with miraculous suddenness the librarian who specialized in murder mysteries and Russian classics, heavily subsidized for the Indian market by the Soviet Union, so that reading Georges Simenon, Agatha Christie, Rex Stout was for us a natural corollary to reading Chekhov, Dostoyevsky, Gorky.

If this meant our tastes were formed by such books as the librarians could buy in secondhand bookshops, it also meant we were uninhibited by literary snobbisms, holding an unshakable belief that any book we borrowed was a potential source of delight and, more important, that there did not exist the book too difficult to read.

The only obstacle to our reading appetites was the tragic absence of a lending library for comics. Alas, the steely-eyed owners of comic-book shops demanded full payment, Cash Down. Such hard-heartedness had enabled them to have permanent establishments— wooden shacks where they sat cross-legged on floors covered with white sheets, smirking at their hoard of treasure. Leaving our shoes on the roadside, we would climb barefoot up the two steps leading into their shops and lose ourselves in a brave new world peopled by Superman, Batman, Scrooge McDuck, Archie and Veronica, Nyoka the Jungle Girl. And of course, those *Classics Illustrated* comics, which would later prove invaluable in getting university degrees in literature because the plots and characters of the West's great novels had been painlessly but indelibly engraved on our brains.

As we grew older, we did of course go to proper bookshops such as the Oxford University Press Book Store on Calcutta's main shopping avenue, Park Street, around the corner from Macaulay's home. The proximity was appropriate. Macaulay had convinced the British government to allow Indians to learn English so that they could become clerks for the British Raj. Leaving the blaring car horns and humidity of Park Street outside, we would enter the cathedral-like store with its glass-fronted bookcases made of rich, polished mahogany, manned by bespectacled assistants whose hushed voices were barely audible over the hum of air-conditioning, and timidly ask for books.

Or in Delhi we would wander through the stucco columns of Lutyens's Connaught Place searching for Ramakrishna and Sons until suddenly, hidden behind the sweeping colonial facades, we would locate the store, piled to the ceiling with tottering pillars of books—and an owner who knew where every title could be found and always had the book you wanted. Or we would browse in Faqir Chand's store in Khan Market because the hunchback owner never let you leave without a monogrammed ballpoint pen or letter opener even if you hadn't bought a book.

In Bombay, beyond the brooding Indo-Saracenic buildings of Bombay University, the Strand Book Stall had a policy of kindness to college students, and a credit line could always be negotiated while advertising executives bought their copies of *Catch-22*.

In these bookstores we struck intellectual attitudes, anxiously awaiting the four new Penguin titles that arrived every month and studying on other Penguins the author photographs of Katherine Anne Porter, Vladimir Nabokov, Nancy Mitford, Evelyn Waugh. Sometimes we abandoned our orange Penguins for the poets published in Faber and Faber's yellow paperbacks. Or clutched the brightly colored American editions of Gertrude Stein, Jack Kerouac, Truman Capote, Nathanael West, which could be so effectively color-coordinated with one's clothes.

Still, our passion for reading was not born in such establishments of visible self-improvement, but in those pavement bookstalls and lending libraries which so tenaciously offered themselves as a necessary adjunct to every pleasure. If you were taken to a restaurant, you had to spend long minutes examining the books spread in front of the entrance. As you did after you had seen a movie. Or been to a cricket match. Or illegally bought a packet of cigarettes. Thus, we were made gluttons for books.

The same gluttony informs my reading today and I remain as indiscriminate now as I was in my childhood. Give me a history or a biography and it will trigger off hours of rumination on human behavior. A contemporary novel to keep in touch with the zeitgeist. A golden oldie because each rereading increases the original passion for the book. Give me a volume of poetry for that kidney punch, what Emily Dickinson called "that turning to ice of the limbs" so essential to the compulsive reader. Or a book on science or philosophy, since who can tell when one might suddenly grasp the Theory of Chaos or Kierkegaard. And give me always a couple of detective novels in case my flight is delayed.

I admit it. I am an addict. Addicted to reading by those pavement magicians shouting at us like circus barkers: those booksellers endlessly rearranging their displays and corrupting us with their seductive litany of titles—as they lured us away from the little world of the self into whole galaxies of the imagination.

28

Indian Decor

At the beginning of this century a young Indian lancer from the kingdom of Jodhpur who had fought against the troops of the Dowager Empress of China in the Boxer Rebellion took some time off for rest and recreation and visited Japan. As he was of noble blood, he was received by the Emperor of Japan at the palace in Kyoto.

The lancer was horrified by the austerity of the ruler of the Chrysanthemum Throne. "Except for a painted screen at the very end of the audience chamber," the lancer noted in his diary, "the audience hall was completely EMPTY."

Such shock on the part of an Indian would have been entirely appropriate, according to William Archer. The British Indologist describes the Indian aesthetic as being one of "gargantuan excess." The lancer might well have understood the Zen principle behind the Emperor of Japan's decor, since Zen is a corruption of the Sanskrit word *dhyan*, meaning "awareness." But to achieve awareness through the contemplation of a solitary object amounts to tunnel vision for an Indian.

Not for Indians the tranquillity of gazing at the glaze on a single perfect pot. We find satisfaction in the glazes on a hundred different pots, in a hundred stages of disintegration. What the West hides in the attic to be examined in moments of nostalgia, Indians keep proudly to hand. On the wall of an Indian home a miniature painted in the sixteenth century by a master artist to the court of a Moghul Emperor will hang next to a group photograph taken to commemorate a meeting with a minor British official during the days of the British Raj, and both will fade into obscurity against the lurid colors of an Indian calendar with its illustrations of voluptuous Indian deities or film stars.

While this makes the Indian home interesting, it also means the Indian home is without a "look" and fails to "make a statement," lacking the discrimination that in Europe and America constitutes an aesthetic.

But then Ananda Coomaraswamy, the great

scribe of Indian culture, is scathing about aesthetics. He dismisses aesthetes as mere effetes, capable only of the passive response. And there is no passivity in the Indian home. It dares to exist in a civilization where eras and cultures are colliding with such force that the home itself is sustained only by an act of will, clinging stubbornly to an idea of order in the midst of disorder, a gallant belief in form in the midst of malfunction.

I once overheard a French lady commiserating with a former Maharajah as he showed her around his palace. "You must be so sad to see it like this," she said sympathetically. "It must have been formidable when it was perfect." Her host looked bewildered—he simply did not understand the sentiment. The Indian home has never been perfect. It is always in a state of decay and reassembly. And in this mobility lies the essential difference between excess in India and excess in the West.

For a start, mobility in the West is directed upward. Increased status and wealth confer the capacity and the necessity for visible improvement, demanding that residences, objects, furniture, paintings, become ever more refined, more exclusive. In short, discrimination is all. But Indians are short of cash. They cannot afford to remake the world closer to the heart's desire. In contrast to the upward mobility of the West, the Indian home has a sort of amoebic mobility capable of assimilating both an individual history and the history of a civilization which, because it cannot afford to throw things away, absorbs them. Or waits for them to fall apart.

The Indian's home is neither his castle nor a stage set designed by his decorator. By necessity it is organic. So travelers to India will be familiar with high-ceilinged rooms that still retain the iron hoops from another century which once held heavy curtains attached by ropes to small boys in adjacent chambers pulling the curtains to stir the summer air. Today, between these hoops there hangs a fan with wide wooden blades where a family of sparrows is nesting—because the noisy air conditioner listing at an awkward angle beneath a carved window has long since rendered both iron hoops and wooden fans obsolete.

If the Indian home has an aesthetic, it is chaos, enabling it to accommodate regional influences as separate in their ways as Spain is from Scandinavia, as well as European influences from the long reign of the British Empire and Islamic influences from eight centuries of Muslim domination. So an average Indian bungalow, for instance, will probably have a pillared verandah: the number of pillars outside a

Hindu home traditionally indicates the eminence of the owner. Well, it did. Until the British imported the aesthetic of Grecian and Roman pillars. Now in your average bungalow, European decoration and Hindu tradition are fused in stucco to support a roof from which is suspended the traditional Indian swing, facing wrought-iron lawn furniture derived from the European gazebo. Above the pseudo-Palladian doorway hangs a garland of holy basil leaves and marigold blossoms to bless the house, and on the un-Indian architrave is precariously balanced an image of the elephant-headed god of protection, Ganesh.

Inside the rooms, wool or silk carpets with Persian motifs will—if it is winter—lie on top of cotton dhurries used in spring, and both are removed during the summer heat to reveal stone or marble floors. Such attention to the ground is inevitable in a culture accustomed to taking off its shoes before entering a room. Then, on the carpets will be a heady variety of furniture—from the bolster-covered platforms on which Indians habitually recline, to the Victorian sofas and chairs on which Englishmen once sat bolt upright, to the Art Deco and Art Nouveau remnants from the days when Indians danced the tango.

Enclosed corridors and walled courtyards indicate the influence of Islam's sequestered women, and in the dining room—a British concept—silver or copper platters holding individual food containers as dictated by Hinduism's caste considerations lie in happy juxtaposition to assorted items of European china.

Over time the architecture and artifacts of alien worlds have been made familiar to India through extended usage. Possessions are not so much displayed as lurking about, waiting to be used—in themselves incontrovertible evidence that when an irresistible force such as life meets any immovable object, something's got to give. In India that something is usually good taste.

So it is no good asking an Indian, "What is that refrigerator doing plugged into that marble wall inlaid with cornelian and lapis lazuli?"

Because the Indian will only look at you as though you were a cretin and answer, "Keeping the water cold."

It was India's greatest filmmaker who summed it all up. Satyajit Ray once said that Indians have an infinite tolerance for decay. Certainly in our homes elements of heartstopping beauty coexist with examples of equally heartstopping awfulness. While such intolerable tolerance occasions distress in the visitor, it seems to leave the locals curiously unfazed. Perhaps this is because the Indian looks on his home more as a place to live than as a work of art. The art, if there is one in India, is supposed to lie in the living.

29

Filming

The year India became a free country the Indian filmmaker Satyajit Ray helped found the Calcutta Film Society. In later years he would celebrate Calcutta, often associated only with beggars and infamous black holes, as Mahanagar, the Great City.

Not that Ray had an easy time filming his celluloid poems of the Great City's anguished humanity. Politicians objected when Ray's films were cleared by the film censor.

"He is painting a bad picture of the nation," they complained. "The world will think we have only poverty."

The politicians needn't have worried. The world wasn't interested. Western distributors found Ray's films too slow and Indian distributors declined to show them because "people come to see films in order to forget their problems. Who wants to see reality on the screen?"

It is true that in avoiding reality Indian cinema audiences have created the largest film industry in the world, most of it based in Bombay, a city that has taken to calling itself, with awful coyness, Bollywood. And Bollywood has given its audiences escape in every form—from religious epics to emotional melodrama to action movies, affectionately known as "curry Westerns," to ghost stories, all filled with the song and dance routines that are an essential part of commercial Indian cinema.

But an industry that learned its craft from the Lumière brothers themselves at the turn of the century, when the men who invented cinematography visited India, has addressed both reality and fantasy in its hundred years of existence. True, the first Indian feature films, made by Dadasaheb Phalke, had mythological themes: *Rajah Harishchandra* in 1913, *The Legend of Krishna* in 1918. But they were designed to make audiences gasp at miraculous moving pictures that could so suspend reality that you could see gods flying high above human beings. As silent movies, they transcended the barrier of India's many languages, and India's common mythology freed the filmmaker to use all the magic of the new technology to make his audience marvel at film's possibilities.

A common mythology has been indispensable to the growth of our cinema. Our movies have been described as folk plays transferred onto celluloid. Both have a familiar array of stock characters, music and dance routines, and plots that mix tragedy with comedy. The formula has allowed films to penetrate into the deepest corners of India, making an alien medium only another vehicle for the familiar.

So in the twenties and thirties, while some Indian directors shot lavish spectaculars and even used foreign actors and European locations, other directors, watched closely by the administrators of the British Raj, used the narrative form of folk drama and seemingly innocuous themes, such as the life of the great singer-saint Meerabai, or the heroic King Prithvi Raj, to make thinly disguised political allegories for an audience fired by nationalist fervor.

When India became free, directors dealing with uncommercial subjects like moneylending and the poverty of Indian farmers still managed to make films of powerful social commentary that were blockbuster successes both at home and abroad, such as *Mother India* and *Do Bigha Zameen*. At the same time, Indian cinema was turning out popular comedies and melodramas that used some of India's most talented musicians and singers to compose film scores and record songs to which actors mouthed the words. Only commercial cinema's dance routines were perforce becoming a little more suggestive. Choreographers had to compensate for the ban on kissing in films imposed by the puritans of the new India. Our film censors had made it official. Kissing was un-Indian.

From the late sixties onward, India was awash in black money, and undeclared cash fortunes found their way into the film industry as a convenient form of money laundering, dictating its new vulgarity. Stars who could pull in an audience were earning huge amounts of money, acting in three or four films simultaneously, rushing from one shoot to another with ever larger entourages. It was the heyday of the curry Western, the superstar, the lush location. Dance sequences that began in the valleys of Kashmir suddenly included an Eiffel Tower or a Trevi Fountain around which the hero and heroine made their voluptuous invitations to each other, although one memorable dance sequence confined itself to the keys of a huge red typewriter.

By the time the industry entered the eighties, our films were unself-consciously ripping off American television serials and flaunting the special effects of wealth. It was no longer wrong to be young, beautiful, Westernized, and bad. Skirts and sequinned gowns appeared on the ladies, leather jackets on the gents. Stars spent more time on motorbikes, in helicopters and speedboats, and less time in the Indian countryside, where eighty percent of their audience lived. And hit movies were made by the suggestiveness of their dance routines, leaving us all longing for the simple days when a kiss was just a kiss, not this pistonlike movement of hips and breasts by fully clothed members of opposing sexes. In Parliament they had hardly noticed that Indian film stars were kissing again. The country's representatives were now trying to control the dancing.

During these two decades, films from a new wave of directors—funded by a newly created government film finance board—bridged the gap between the fantasies of commercial cinema and the daily events of ordinary Indian lives.

But one group of young filmmakers from Kerala wanted to avoid accepting government largesse, with its inevitable corollary, government interference. This left them with the problem of raising on their own the seemingly impossible sums required to pay for film stock, actors, cameras, cameramen, lights, soundmen, costumes, sets, laboratories, editing studios.

For weeks they debated the best means of

funding their projects. Finally they came up with the novel notion of screening films in villages for a fee. Hiring a van and a projector, they sent out word to the Kerala villages that they would be holding film shows for which they would make the nominal charge of one rupee, the equivalent of three cents. The excited population of whole villages crowded into rice fields for the great event. The cinema was actually coming to them, at a price even they could afford.

"How long did it take to earn the finance for your film?" I asked one of the directors, Adoor Gopalakrishanan, at a festival where his film was being shown.

"About a year and a half."

"That's all? Did you expect to do it so quickly?"

"We kept our costs low and rented movies from the film societies."

"What did you make those poor villagers watch?"

"Eisenstein and De Sica. Resnais. Pabst. Kurosawa."

We both knew that most of the villagers at the screenings had never been to a town, let alone seen any pictures of the outside world. Now they were being forced to sit through those lengthy film classics, shot in black and white.

"Did they like anything?"

"Of course. Why not? Indian villagers can understand the story of *The Seven Samurai* better than you or me. They enjoyed *The Bicycle Thief* also. Only, they hated *Hiroshima, Mon Amour*. Catcalls and boos, I'm afraid."

Hiroshima, Mon Amour. I tried to visualize all that French world-weariness being projected in an open field—with no electricity for miles around, with cattle lowing and pi-dogs barking—for the delight of a village audience.

"Did they have a favorite?"

"We gave many repeat performances of Eisenstein's *Battleship Potemkin*. If you ask me, their taste is better than the audience at this film festival."

His story reminded me of Louis Malle's experience while filming in Calcutta. Malle had been inspired to make a series of documentaries after seeing the film about India made by Roberto Rossellini in the fifties. A friend of mine, Santi Choudhary, who had been Satyajit Ray's partner for several years but now had his own film production company, was working with Malle.

Malle's filming was halted one day by a huge demonstration against the government. Passions were running high and the crowds were expected to swell to half a million people. The police had put out radio bulletins advising people to stay in their homes, not to attend their offices—in fact, not to venture out at all unless they had urgent business.

Determined to capture this event on film, Malle prevailed upon Santi to take him to the Maidan, Calcutta's central park, where the demonstration was to take place. Warning Malle the crowds would turn hostile if they saw cameras and sound equipment, somehow Santi maneuvered the film van into the center of the demonstration. As Santi had predicted, when tanned Frenchmen wearing safari suits and loaded with film equipment began exiting the van, an agitated Calcutta traffic policeman pushed his way toward them, gesticulating wildly. "Get away! Go please! Big strike! Unsafe! Bad for foreigner!"

Santi heaved himself out of the van and whispered conspiratorially into the policeman's ear. "Can't you let us stay? This is the great French filmmaker Louis Malle."

The cynical ploy worked better than he had expected. The traffic policeman clapped his hands in delight. "Louis Malle? Louis Malle himself? But I have seen his films and read all about him in *Cahiers du Cinéma*. Please translate. Ask what he personally thinks of the work of Jean-Luc Godard."

As Santi pointed out later, if the traffic policeman's facility with language wasn't up to conversing with Louis Malle in English, how had he ever managed to understand *Cahiers du Cinéma*? That bible of cineastes was published only in French. The policeman probably had a salary of forty dollars a month, but he told Santi he had somehow scraped enough money together to become a member of the Calcutta Film Society. Now here he was in the middle of a Calcutta demonstration, described by international journalists as among the most potentially violent situations in the world, happily discussing the minutiae of French New Wave cinema with a French director.

But then, as Satyajit Ray has shown the world through his films, Calcutta is Mahanagar, the Great City, whose citizens manage to dream under the most oppressive conditions. And as the traffic policeman proves, their dreams are not necessarily the dreams that come out of the fantasy factories of Bollywood.

Maybe that was why they reacted as they did when a tearful radio announcer told his city that their ailing filmmaker, Satyajit Ray, had died. People poured out of their homes. Offices closed down. The government was brought to a standstill as bureaucrats deserted their desks.

During his lifetime this giant of the cinema

always had to beg for money to make his next film. In a career spanning forty years, budget limitations seldom allowed him to film more than two takes of any scene, no matter how complicated, forcing him to draw each frame of his scripts meticulously by hand so that he could shoot in a series of single takes. He composed the music, wrote the dialogue, designed the sets, directed the action, edited the rushes for films like *Mahanagar* and the *Apu* trilogy and *Charulata* and *The Music Room*. When they were screened at film festivals around the world, he was acknowledged as a master of his form. But distributors and backers in India were adamant: "Your films will only lose money. We want films that give Indians the chance to escape the drudgery of their lives."

Before his own government honored him, he was honored many times abroad, and even as he lay dying in hospital, the President of France awarded him France's Légion d'Honneur and Hollywood, not Bollywood, gave him a lifetime achievement award for his contribution to cinema.

Yet India's distributors called him a financial loser, called his work of interest to the very few. They said they knew their audience. Did they? Learning of his death, in a spontaneous display of grief six hundred thousand people came out on the streets of Calcutta to pay silent homage to Satyajit Ray as his body was driven to its cremation.

Has any audience anywhere in the world given any filmmaker such an accolade?

30

Communications

One Sunday morning in 1996 I was glancing through an Indian newspaper and chanced upon a mirror of contemporary India. These stories were adjacent on the front page.

A telecommunications company had just concluded its negotiations and was in a position to offer Indians who owned personal computers a facility to access Web sites in two hundred and thirty countries. This was quite handy, as Indians had begun placing matrimonial advertisements in the electronic marketplace.

No longer limited to the Indian Sunday newspapers, now readers around the world could respond to:

Government Contractor Builder seeks alliance with fair beautiful sharp featured girl from educated status family. Correspond with bio-data.

Or: *Compatible Bride wanted for Associate Professor. Early decent marriage.*

Or: *Foreign Qualified Architect invites alliance from slim fair charming modest soft-spoken well-mannered adjustable-natured sitar-playing sociable humorous cultural broad-minded honest loyal with clean past conversational English preferably architect or civil engineer bride.*

Luckily for his future bride, this demanding bridegroom had added: *Religion Caste Faith No Bar.* There has been a dramatic change in matrimonial demands in the last few years. Fewer advertisements require the same caste or religious faith, or object to previous marriages. The essential requirements for both sexes seem to be professional and educational qualifications. And a large number of advertisements are from people with M.B.A. degrees from Western universities who are living abroad. In fact, the newspaper columns are now headlined by professional status: DOCTORS. CIVIL SERVANTS. M.B.A./ C.A. NON RESIDENT INDIANS. OTHER FOREIGNERS. So it is common to find advertisements for:

Wanted Beautiful Vegetarian Convented Medico Match for Smart Handsome M.D. Radio-Diagnosis No Bars.

Or: *American white male 35 years sincere honest looks for Indian wife.*

Or: *Distinguished Decorated Handsome Army Captain seeks Convent-Educated Wife Serving Army Doctors Preferred: Caste, Widow No Bar.*

The willingness to marry widows is particularly poignant because the next column in the newspaper carried an article on sati—the vile practice where Hindu widows burned themselves alive on their husbands' funeral pyres.

Although sati has been illegal in India for nearly two centuries, in 1987 in the western Indian state of Rajasthan an eighteen-year-old widow who had been married only eight months committed suicide by burning herself on her husband's pyre in full view of her whole village and thousands of spectators from nearby villages. The local authorities had looked the other way on the grounds that they could not have prevented it.

"After all, she was a Rajput girl," they said.

There was indeed a historical tradition of Rajput women burning themselves on their husbands' pyres, especially when a battle had been lost and they stood the chance of being taken prisoner. Treated as saints for their act of devotion, their cenotaphs were places of pilgrimage, mostly to other women desperate to give their husbands sons. In fact, the young widow had burned herself on a pyre next to the cenotaphs of three earlier satis of the village.

The authorities had hoped rather too optimistically that the whole sorry business of this modern sati would remain a local secret. But the story of a new saint spread like wildfire, drawing legions of pilgrims who required soft drinks, souvenirs, food, garlands of flowers, and incense to place at the spot where the sati had burned herself, as well as the opportunity of hearing accounts of her life from people who knew her when she was a mere mortal, accounts of miracles witnessed since she became immortal.

Local politicians rushed to the spot, eager for self-promotion. Some argued such acts of heroism symbolized all that placed the Rajput woman so far above her Indian sisters. Others wanted the officials, the woman's family, and the watching villagers tried as accessories to murder.

Journalists and women's rights groups descended on the village from all over India. *Can you imagine that her act of sati was voluntary?* the women's groups shouted. Even if she had gone willingly, she was only a young girl trying to escape the cruelties still practiced against rural widows, forced to cut off their hair, living like slaves on the charity of their in-laws.

I knew what they meant. I had once shared a railway carriage filled with young women with shorn heads, their bare shoulders and shins exposed by saris once white but now gray with coal dust from the engines. They looked like children with their long, vulnerable necks, these village widows on their way to Varanasi to cover their shoulders with cotton scarves printed with the prayer *Hari Krishna Hari Ram*, which they would recite for their dead husbands as they begged in the streets until they themselves died of starvation.

Meanwhile, the journalists in Rajasthan were asking: Had the woman been forced into burning herself by the avarice of her husband's family, trying to earn a supplementary income? Or was it a plot in which all the villagers were involved? Would other village women be forced to do the same thing?

A reporter who had visited the area told me later she had interviewed the village women. "I was quite surprised. When I inquired if any of them were likely to commit sati, they said, 'Only if our husbands agree to burn themselves on our funeral pyres if we die first.'"

Under the glare of the entire nation's attention, the local authorities panicked and had the building of a temple stopped, forbidding the villagers any further exploitation of the young widow's death.

Now, ten years later, an enterprising young journalist had decided to revisit the area just to see how things had progressed. He found people were still placing flower garlands on the site of the immolation. Television antennae waved above the village huts. This struck the journalist as particularly horrible. He was convinced the profits from an ancient and cruel practice had taken this village into the world of global communications, the revenues still keeping the village there.

Between the articles on Web sites and sati was a picture of a young man with earrings and shoulder-length hair.

The accompanying story informed us that a young Indian rock star had arrived in town from London and the music he was playing to packed halls was a hybrid of Western and Eastern tunes called Indi-pop. The photograph made him look like a Native American warrior. But we were told there was already an Indi-pop star—or was it a Raga-rap star?—called Apache Indian. Still, the earrings framing the singer's clean features and strong brown face were similar to those worn by many Indian farmers. Perhaps he should have been playing Bhangra-rock, that other Indian music craze, which combined the insistent drumbeats of a northern harvest dance with the equally insistent beat of rock and roll.

Anyway, there was no reason for him to be self-conscious about his appearance. The audience of young girls dancing to his music were themselves dressed in hybrid forms—saris and miniskirts, anklets and Doc Martens boots, salwar kameezes and torn Levi's—enjoying a brief fling with freedom before the restrictions of Indian society overwhelmed their lives.

One of the songs such audiences had already made into a huge hit had the evocatively Indian name "Arranged Marriage."

31

Trees

In India when a boy and girl get engaged, their horoscopes are read by the family priest to see if the couple are compatible. But astrological compatibility extends far beyond whether the young man and the young woman will suit each other. The priests of India are supremely uninterested as to whether Darby finds his Joan or Abélard his Héloïse. They are searching for the wider significance of the union.

"When this girl marries into our family," the bridgroom's parents ask their priest, "will she bring us luck? Will she increase our wealth or will she cast a shadow over our house, perhaps shortening her mother-in-law's life or bringing bad health to her father-in-law?"

If the girl's horoscope reveals the faintest

hint of such possibilities, the priest shakes his head and informs the prospective in-laws, "It is very sad but you have chosen a *manglik* girl to be your son's wife."

Happily for the *manglik* girl, she is not doomed by a fate over which she has no control to the life of a frustrated spinster. There is a solution to her problem. She must first marry someone else, transferring her ill fortune to another husband. Then, purified, she can finally marry her original bridegroom secure in the knowledge that she is bringing only good luck to his house.

But which husband is so noble that he will marry this unfortunate girl first and take upon himself her ill-starred destiny, only to release her, cleansed, into the arms of another man? Travelers in India will have passed trees with withered flower garlands hanging from their branches. Those garlands denote the presence of a husband. The *manglik* girl garlands a tree as her bridegroom in a marriage ceremony as elaborate as that between human beings—to cleanse herself of the misfortunes of her fate. And of course, if it is the prospective bridegroom who is the *manglik*, then he takes a tree as his first wife.

The use of trees to receive evil is an idea as old as India itself. The devout still believe the tree is all that remains on earth of the sacred soma plant, which provides nourishment to the gods themselves. The Atharva-Veda, written a thousand years before the birth of Christ, contains the prayer

> *The sin, the pollution,*
> *Whatever we have done with evil,*
> *With your leaves we wipe it off.*

Is it any wonder, then, that the tree is sacred to India. Or the forest a *tirth*, a place of pilgrimage as holy as any temple.

To the artists of India the tree has an even greater significance. They believe the tree gifted art to mankind. The Puranas, texts of the oldest Indian legends, tell the story thus: the gods had become quarrelsome and Vac, Sacred Speech, fled the profaning gods to hide in water. When the vengeful gods claimed her, the intimidated waters gave her up. So Sacred Speech fled the waters and took sanctuary in a forest. Again the gods claimed her, but the trees refused to surrender her to the spiteful gods. Instead, the trees gave Vac to man in offerings made of wood: the flute, the drum, the lute, the pen. With these, men were instructed to tell of the Creation.

Then there is the tree and Indian philosophy. To the philosophers of ancient India the forest was the symbol of an idealized cosmos. The great Indian philosophical academies were all held in groves of trees, an acknowledgment that the forest—self-sufficient, endlessly regenerative—combined in itself the diversity and the harmony that were the aspiration, the goal of Indian metaphysics. It is not by chance that out of India's forests came the great body of India's knowledge: the Puranas, the Vedas, the Upanishads, the epics of the *Mahabharata* and the *Ramayana*, the Yoga sutras, and the medical studies of the Ayurveda.

Inevitably, such veneration of the forest had its impact on the city. Following the geometry of Indian philosophy, the Indian city had at its heart a grove of trees from which the streets emanated outward like branches—to remind the city dwellers that man is only one part of an enormous living organism. And when townsfolk had fulfilled their obligations to the material life of the city—marriage, children, governance, war, trade, pleasure—they retreated to the forest to end their lives in contemplation and meditation, drawing from trees the tranquillity necessary to such reflection.

Again, it is not by chance that the Buddha and Mahavira, the founders of Buddhism and Jainism, two of India's great religions, should both have attained enlightenment not on the road to some Damascus but while meditating under a tree.

The Indian Nobel Laureate, the poet Rabindranath Tagore, attempted to explain the essential silviculture of India in his book *Tapovan:*

> Indian civilisation has been distinctive in locating its source of regeneration, material and intellectual, in the forest not the city. India's best ideas have come when man was in communion with trees. Indian thinkers were surrounded by and linked to the life of the forest, and the intimate relationship between human life and living nature became the source of their knowledge.

It is as if, over thousands of years, India has woven a mantle of conservation around herself with threads of morality, art, philosophy, religion, mythology. Especially mythology.

Trees feature in so much Indian mythology—providing shade or sanctuary to the divine—they have become sacred in themselves. The goddess Meenakshi resides in the forest at Madurai, a grove sacred twice over because it is also the playground of the god Krishna and his adoring milkmaids. In Kanchi, the god Shiva, creator and destroyer of worlds, once appeared to a sage sitting under a mango tree. That mango grove became a pilgrimage center, all mango trees considered sacred since.

Throughout India trees are worshipped as incarnations of the Goddess. Bamani, Rupeshwari, Vandurga are the divinities who reveal themselves to men in the guise of such trees as the saal, the deodar, the banyan. And Aranyani, goddess of the forest, has inspired a whole body of texts known as Aranyani Sanskriti, which translates as "the civilization of the forest."

That civilization was founded by India's first inhabitants, and it is still followed by their descendants. In tribal India the tree is venerated as the earth mother, not only because it provides food, air, nourishment, occupation, materials for housing and fodder and fuel, but because without the tree there is neither soil nor water—nothing to prevent the one from being washed away, the other from evaporating. In the great tribal tracts of India—home to the Bhils, the Santals, the Nagas, the Bishnois—whenever a child is born, a tree is planted in the child's name, forging a relationship between child and tree closer than the one between child and family because that tree is uniquely the child's. The trees are all slow-growing, and by the time the child reaches adolescence, his tree has just come into fruit, commencing its life as provider to the tribal and the tribal's life as guardian of the tree.

The forest, then, is India's central metaphor for the Creation, venerated as a symbol of inexhaustible fertility, represented again and again in Indian art as the tree of life, referred to again and again in Indian literature as a paradigm of the cosmos.

So, with all this veneration, this adoration, this reproduction in art, literature, and philosophy, it seems beyond belief that in the last century Indians could have permitted half the country's trees to be cut down by the administrators of the British Empire to make way for railways and mines, and then, during the last thirty years, themselves cut down half of the remaining half.

The Hindu scriptures tell us that we are living in Kalyug—the Age of Evil, the Era of Immorality. And the characteristic evil of our evil age is speed. Even so, the statistics of what is happening to the subcontinent's forest cover are shocking proof of the velocity of our immorality.

Of the thousands of miles of dense virgin jungle that covered the great range of the Nepal Himalayas as recently as 1950, it is calculated that if commercial felling continues at the present rate, there will not be a single tree left by the end of the century.

Logging and stone quarrying have destroyed the forest cover of the Indian Himalayas with equal devastation. We know the impact this is having on the monsoon rains, which are life or death to the subcontinent, and yet we watch complacently while the denuding of the Himalayan forests leads to a cycle of flood, drought, homelessness, and hunger that repeats itself with increasing speed as our glaciers retreat and our topsoil is washed away and our waters evaporate because there is nothing to retain them.

And each year we see the price of our indifference exacted from the rice fields of Bangladesh as swollen rivers burst their banks with such frequency that the world is now inured to the thought that each year in Bangladesh another half a million people will lose their lands, their livelihoods, perhaps even their lives.

By replacing veneration of the tree with consumption of the tree, it is as if the subcontinent is no longer able to connect cause with effect.

The sages sitting in the forests of ancient India reciting the Puranas may have had some presentiment of the India that was to come. The Puranic legend says the marauding gods were enraged when the forest refused to surrender Sacred Speech to them and gave her instead to man as instruments of music and literature. In their anger the gods placed a fearful curse upon all trees: "Because through instruments of wood you have given what is sacred to mankind, so again with instruments made of your bodies, with axes with wooden handles, as thunderbolts will men cut you down."

Nearly three hundred years ago men and women of the Bishnoi tribe died in an attempt to end that curse. The Bishnoi faith prohibits the cutting of green trees and demands absolute protection of the khejari, the shade and fodder tree of the area. As a result, their lands are still fertile, while all around them fields have been reclaimed by the Thar Desert of Rajasthan. Although in earlier centuries other members of the Bishnoi tribe gave their lives to protect their trees, the story most often told describes the martyrdom of Amrita Devi—a woman from a Bishnoi village in the kingdom of Jodhpur.

Amrita Devi, like her fellow tribals, had been raised to love and tend the trees that encircled her village. So when the axmen of the Jodhpur King—needing timber for the royal lime kilns—arrived to chop down the trees, Amrita Devi confronted the axmen and begged them to leave the forest untouched. She explained the religious beliefs of the Bishnois. The King's axmen were unmoved. As they unsheathed their axes, Amrita Devi flung her arms around the first tree marked for felling. The blades sliced through her body, and as she bled to death, she uttered the words that have become a slogan of her tribe: "A chopped head is still easier to replace than a chopped tree."

Then Amrita Devi's daughter took the place of her dismembered mother. She too was killed, only to be replaced by a younger sister, who, in dying, yielded her place to the third and youngest sister, who also gave her life trying to protect the tree with her body. Throughout that day unarmed men, women, and children from eighty-three surrounding Bishnoi villages converged on Amrita Devi's village to protect the trees, but the axmen continued to relentlessly fell the trees and their protectors. By nightfall nearly four hundred tribals from separate Bishnoi villages had been butchered. Like Amrita Devi and her daughters, whole families had died in defense of the khejari forest.

There is an annual fair still held in commemoration of those deaths in Amrita Devi's village. A regular visitor to this fair is a man named Sunderlal Bahuguna, whom many Indians revere as the Mahatma of India's Forests. He calls the fair "my one important place of pilgrimage"—because it is the method first used by the Bishnoi tribe, that he emulated in the Chipko Movement to save what remains of the Himalayan forest.

The word *chipko* means "to cling," and throughout the Himalayas villagers and conservationists, students and folk poets, are attempting to halt India's deforestation by clinging to trees marked for felling by commercial contractors. The Chipko Movement is also planting trees, fighting to replace the monocultural forests of fast-growing trees—like the eucalyptus and the pine intended for the wood pulp industry and which give nothing to the soil or to the people who live off the soil—with the great, slow-growing trees and the mixed forests on which so much of India's economy and ecological balance depends.

The Chipko Movement has now spread from the Himalayas to southern India, where ten years ago a group of peasants—men and women—marched en masse to a government nursery and uprooted thousands of eucalyptus seedlings, planting tamarind and mango seeds in their place, protesting that these trees, not the eucalyptus, keep the soil and its people alive. Of course, they were thrown in jail, while Indian newspapers continued to carry full-page advertisements for just such government nurseries, heavily supported incidentally by the progressive officials of the World Bank, who urged Indians to invest in eucalyptus. MONEY GROWS ON TREES! the newspaper advertisements shrieked.

EARN GREEN GOLD! Sometimes trees were not mentioned at all, merely wealth: BUMPER PROFITS WILL BE YOURS!

The officials who run these nurseries, as indeed their colleagues in the World Bank, would not pass the test of good government described in a folktale of the Santal tribes who live in Bengal and Orissa.

Once upon a time, the story goes, there was a king who had many reservoirs and around the edges of the water he planted trees: mangoes, peepuls, palm trees, banyan trees. And the banyans were bigger than any of the other trees. And every day after his bath the king used to walk about and look at the trees. And one morning as he did so he saw a maiden go up to a banyan and climb it, and as soon as she was safely in its branches, the tree was carried up into the sky. But when the king went back to the same spot in the evening, he saw the tree back in its place again.

The same thing happened three or four days in a row. The king told no one what he had seen, but one morning he climbed the banyan before the maiden appeared. When she clambered up its branches, he was carried up to the sky along with the maiden.

In the sky the maiden descended from the tree and went to dance with a group of celestial milkmaids. So the king also got down and joined in the dance. He was so absorbed he took no notice of the time. And when at last he tore himself away, he found that the banyan tree had disappeared. There was nothing to be done but stay in the sky.

So he began to wander about heaven and soon he came to some men building a palace as quickly as they could. He asked for whom the palace was being built and the men said, "For you. Because you are a good ruler who plants trees for your subjects so they will have food and shelter long after you have gone." Suddenly the banyan reappeared, so the king climbed back up into it and was carried safely back to earth.

After that, the king used to visit the banyan every day, and when he found it did not wither—although it had been taken up to the sky by its roots—he concluded that what he had seen was true. He began to prepare for death, making no answer to the questions of his courtiers as he distributed all his wealth among his subjects. A few days later he died and was taken to the palace he had seen being built in the sky.

Because, it is said by us Santals, the trees you have tended in this world will bring you honor in the next world and all the worlds beyond.

I can't help agreeing with the Santals. Planting a tree does indeed bring honor to those who do so—including all those politicians who plant trees with fixed smiles on their faces while the world's cameras record their exertions. But as an Indian I know there is more than honor in the act.

For us the preservation of trees is as much a matter of cultural as of ecological survival. The forests of India have been the cradle, the university, the monastery, the library of Indian civilization. By exchanging our essential love of the tree—which gave us a view of the world in which man and nature were dependent on each other—for a Western culture that has made man the monarch and the consumer of nature, clearing forests first for agriculture and then for industry, we are exchanging our capacity to understand the relationship between living things for a purely linear, purely profit-oriented view of the world.

And for a more precise understanding of what such a view means to the world, we have only to listen to the alarm expressed by the astronauts circling the globe. They tell us they can no longer see Earth from space. Our planet is now obscured by smoke from Siberia to Brazil, rising from the funeral pyres of our great forests.

India has traditionally prided herself on being Karma Bhoomi—the Land of Experience—

dismissing other countries as lands of the consumer. It is true that from the folktales of her tribals to the monumental works that are the pillars of Indian civilization, India has no shortage of experience to help the world find a balance between man's technology and the earth on which he wields it.

But if the curse of the Puranas has found its time and Indians persist—like thunderbolts—in slaughtering their trees, then we will become a people ever more deracinated. We will, quite literally, cut ourselves off from our cultural and philosophical roots by the action of cutting down our trees.

32

Love Song of India

In the twelfth century the poet Jayadeva sang India's greatest love song outside the Jagannath Temple in the holy city of Puri so that passing strangers, forbidden entrance to the temple, could also listen to the trysts and deceptions, the separations and consummations, described in the *Gita Govinda*.

The Jagannath Temple is one of the holiest places of pilgrimage in India because it is home to the last benign incarnation of the god Vishnu. When this epoch is over, Vishnu will incarnate into Kalki and destroy the world.

In possession of such a valuable treasure, the priests of Jagannath are among the most ruthless in India. Only Hindus belonging to the higher castes may enter the temple. And yet

Krishna, an earlier incarnation of Vishnu, is gained not by caste but by bhakti, the ecstatic love of the god felt by devotees who hope to die with his name on their lips. Pushing forward in the crush to touch the idol when the god is carried in procession through the streets of Puri, many devotees have been ground to death under the unstoppable momentum of the chariot's huge wooden wheels, giving the word "juggernaut" to the English language.

Now, standing before the Jagannath Temple, where all could hear the *Gita Govinda*, Jayadeva sang of the milkmaid Radha's adoration for a beautiful young cowherd with a dark complexion and a perfect body, who plays haunting music on his flute and seduces every milkmaid, breaking Radha's heart even as he increases the intensity of her desire. The cowherd is the divine Krishna, and in erotic images of breathtaking sensuality Radha makes love to Krishna in Jayadeva's *Song of God.*

There is a stone slab in the dusty ground in front of the temple to commemorate that moment when low-caste Hindus, Muslims, Buddhists, Jains, who could not enter the temple, all listened to Jayadeva sing of Radha's longing for the adulterous Krishna in some of the most sublime poetry ever written. They heard Radha's aching request to her companion to find this god who came to her bed marked with scratches from the embraces of other women, and the constant refrain of her shameless plea, "Oh friend, make him make love to me."

They listened to the sexual desire that made her escape home to wander through the dangerous jungles of the night to keep a tryst with the god who did not come and did not come while she waited in a fever of longing and fear, and when he finally appeared his body was streaked with another woman's collyrium and sandalwood paste, and he lied to her and still she trembled when he touched her.

Everyone who heard it became intoxicated by Jayadeva's ecstasy, even the listening king of Puri, who traditionally paid temple girls to perform devotional dances and songs in the temple precincts. Now the intoxicated king decreed that the singers sing the *Gita Govinda* in the temple every day at dawn and at dusk. The lord had to be awakened by hearing this divine song. It had to be the last sound the god heard before he slept.

The love song spread through India like fire, adding a new dimension to the mythology of Krishna. Indian history is full of these bhakti movements, great waves of spiritual ecstasy that break the hold of social and religious exclusion, to sweep every section of Indian society into the embrace of an all-inclusive passion. Poets and singers lost in their ecstatic songs have, century after century, mobilized millions of people to break the boundaries of social separation. But nowhere has bhakti been so perfectly stated as in the *Gita Govinda*, which Jayadeva sang in the holy city of Puri, expressing through Radha's lips his own longing for union with his god.

Eight centuries after Jayadeva sang his ecstasy to passing strangers, I went to the Jagannath Temple hoping to hear the temple singers sing his song when the god was put to sleep for the night, only to be told that the temple trust had been taken over by the government and there were no provisions for singers anymore.

Then a priest remembered that the last of the temple singers was still around. After many messages of entreaty she reluctantly agreed to come to the temple and sing the *Gita Govinda* a final time.

At eleven o'clock that night I entered the temple and made my way past the mighty tower with its circling erotic sculptures into the main hall. It was a warm evening and people were sitting on the ground talking to each other or prostrating themselves or telling their beads while children ran around with fresh flower garlands dangling from their fingers. Older people with austere features recited their mantras, holding in their laps leaves containing hibiscus and marigold blossoms and pieces of coconut as offerings to the god and his family. It was the usual combination of gregarious socializing and private worship that goes on in any Indian temple. At the back of the hall I found an old woman of about seventy years with a broken leg, lying full-length on her back, resting her head in her daughter's lap. The priest accompanying me whispered that this was the singer, but she was in such obvious discomfort I hesitated to disturb her and she acknowledged my greeting perfunctorily, turning her head away.

Hidden behind the huge doors that separated the inner sanctum from the main hall were the idols of the gods. While we waited for the doors to open, I sat on the ground watching the children crawling around their mothers on the stone floor and thought about the temple tower outside, with its sculptures locked in blissful copulation, wondering why Indians are able to look at these stone carvings without giggling but the most sophisticated Westerner, accustomed to pornographic television channels and sexually provocative advertisements, is overcome by self-consciousness. Was it the guiltless delight of the sculptures that made the visitor self-conscious?

A sudden clanging of bells interrupted my musings. The doors of the inner sanctum were flung open and the gods were revealed, wooden idols with totemic shapes from India's original tribal culture, which the new religions had not been able to subjugate, only to absorb.

In the presence of the gods the atmosphere in the hall became electric, charged with devotional intensity. People were singing and chanting prayers, their voices rising in a kind of urgency as they moved toward the railing that separated them from the sanctum. I saw the old temple singer limping forward.

The priests cleared a space in the crowd so that she could face the gods. Hands folded, eyes closed, she began to sing. Her voice was cracked and unmelodious. She could not manage the exacting rhythm, the precision of expression, the changing ragas conveying different moods, required by the *Gita Govinda.*

The priests quickly lost interest in her attempt to send the gods to bed with the sublime song soothing their dreams, and plunged the hall in darkness. The scent of burning camphor filled the hall. The old singer's voice petered out in confusion as the priests began circling the deities with their lamps and pressing food that had first been offered to the gods into the hands of the crowds mobbing them, swiftly seizing the money offered in exchange.

The old singer limped out of the hall, leaning

on her daughter's shoulder, obviously irritated at my romantic fantasies, which had brought her out of the comfort of her home. As she grudgingly accepted the money I pressed into her fingers, I realized her irritation was justified.

In the reality of modern India, Indian sexuality is increasingly dictated by Western fashion, and the sensual and sexual confidence that created India's majestic erotic monuments has now been replaced by packaged fantasies.

Young Indians, given access to MTV and its Easternized versions when India opened up to cable television in 1990, have begun styling themselves after the sexual and romantic practices of the mean streets of America or Europe, while lower down the ladder of wealth, where the social mores of traditional Indian society deny easy intercourse between the sexes until after marriages arranged by parents, proliferating publications suggest that the more urbanized the Indian, the more repressed his sexuality.

A new phenomenon is spreading from India's smallest towns to her largest cities—sex by advertisement. In the last two or three years there has been a steady increase in new magazines—with such names as *Broad-Minded* and *Pussy-Cat*—that carry articles on Mother Teresa next to pages and pages and pages of ads from all over India.

The advertisements are for group sex with strangers: *KGB secrecy assured/expected.*

Introductions to the world of sex: *Do you wish to taste the forbidden fruit? Shy and reserved young girls welcome.*

The longing for experience: *First Timer, Virgin, Very Lonely to Be Loved, Having Unique Fantasies.*

Or the frisson of safe adultery: *Are you a lonely housewife? I can arrange a broad-minded meeting place. Two housewives can jointly contact for mutual fun and enjoyment.*

We may be the land of the *Kama Sutra,* that great text on sexuality written by a celibate sage; we may have the Black Pagoda of Konarak with its twenty-foot-high statues locked in consummation; we may worship Shiva in his phallic form and place garlands on the yoni of the Goddess, but today we answer such advertisements as: *Well Educated Mature Hygiene-Conscious Couple Broad-Minded Fun-Loving, Interested to Meet Ladies, Men, Couples. Should Be Well Mannered, Decent. Strict Confy [confidence] Assured.*

Or: *First Timer Couple She Bi, He Well Hung.*

And promises, promises: *Baby It's Your Lucky Day—Handsome Smart Guy—Terribly Exhausting.*

Come back, Jayadeva. India needs another *Gita Govinda.*

Can't you see the whole country is heaving, unfulfilled, telling strangers in magazines, "Oh friend, make him make love to me"?

33

The Old Ways

Several thousand years ago the greatest sages in India, communicating with each other through their telepathic powers, agreed to consider the human condition, and so they levitated to a cave in the Himalayas for a summit of wisdom and ended up producing the science known as the Ayurveda, the Knowledge of Life.

From their own lengthy meditations the sages of the Ayurveda had perceived that Time was Maya, the great play of illusions that disguised the eternal energy of the universe. They also knew that men feared time, because of all living things, only humans were aware of their own mortality. Now the sages asked themselves how humans, in their constant state of agitated activity, could acquire the concentration to discover the universal life force that alone could help them realize their eternal selves and cure their fear of time.

Put another way, how could men find the energy to be still? It is the paradox that informs every aspect of Indian thought, and over centuries many Indian disciplines have evolved to help mankind find the poise and balance necessary for stillness.

For the ear there is the recitation of mantras, or sacred syllables. Whatever religious significance is imputed to them, mantras are only a series of sounds and chanting them is an attempt to still the mind by constant repetition, a method that crosses over into Indian music, which uses a single scale as its mantra, endlessly developing that scale to produce a meditative state in which both musician and audience are lifted beyond pleasure into contemplation.

For the eyes there are the Mandalas, circular forms and representational figures, and there are the Yantras, geometric patterns that purport to carry the secret codes of existence. Ignore their mystical claims and they remain visual aids, created as a meditation for the eyes. Their patterns have found their way into Indian textiles and crafts. Their colors have defined the psychological states induced by Indian painting.

The entire body is the province of the science

of Yoga. The epigrams of the sage Patanjali identify asanas, or postures, in a system of physical disciplines designed to release energy. The last and greatest practice of Yoga is controlled breathing because breath is the origin of life. Those yogis who have mastered that discipline are able to slow down their breathing to such an extent it is almost death, eliminating the separation between man's concept of life and that which is always living.

The whole human being is the focus of the Ayurveda, which holds that human suffering takes three forms—physical, mental, spiritual. To alleviate the body's ills, the Ayurveda has compiled a vast encyclopedia of healing plants, many discovered by the original inhabitants of India's forests and mountains, her tribal population. For the suffering mind the Ayurveda prescribes a variety of meditations to enable a patient to achieve harmony with himself and control his destructive restlessness. And for the Ayurveda's final and greatest concern, the health of a man's soul, the sages state no man can be free of suffering unless he understands the interdependence of all life.

To help man exist in the external world, we have the Vastushastra, the body of Indian treatises on architecture. Vastu starts from the premise that the original act of architecture is the earth, home to all forms of life. When a house is built, certain rituals must acknowledge this fact. The foundations of a house are an invasion of the earth and so the architect must place in the foundations seeds and roots to resow the earth. The raising of the house's central beam is commemorated with another ritual to remind man of a past in which the tree provided the support on which he placed leaves or skins to create his first microcosmic habitation within the wider habitation of the earth.

The house's architecture must acknowledge those elements from which life is composed—earth, air, water, fire, energy. In its ideal construction it should be a series of buildings containing space, opening into a series of courtyards that are pure space in which the elements may move freely, as they do upon the earth, and the house should have a pavilion, containing space while still remaining space, to allow the energies of the earth's magnetic fields to enter from all sides. Instructions on the planting of gardens and trees, as well as the alignment of water bodies and the necessity to keep water and air free of pollution, treat the act of building as the creation of a living thing.

Mantras, Mandalas, Yoga, have always been

used in India as routes to self-realization. Today Ayurvedic practices and Vastu are staging a vigorous comeback, a sign that Indians are at last acquiring the confidence to examine their own knowledge in order to find answers to their problems. Unfortunately, much of the current interest in Vastu is based on a superstitious belief that a house which observes Vastu tenets can harness energies which will bring wealth or good fortune to the owner. And more and more books on the Ayurveda are concerned with beauty aides, reducing a concept of the universe as a harmonious whole to the preoccupations of narcissism.

Even the contemplations that are supposed to lead to an understanding of the unifying principles of life have so often been used selfishly that India's Nobel Laureate, the poet Rabindranath Tagore, raged, "Alas my cheerless country, dressed in worn-out rags, loaded with decrepit wisdom. You pride yourself on having seen through the fraud of creation. Sitting idly in your corner, all you do is sharpen the edge of your metaphysical mumbo-jumbo . . ."

I think Tagore was a bit harsh, but our piecemeal practices of a unifying philosophy have indeed fragmented a once intact vision of the world in which man is the guardian of a living organism, responsible for seeing its fragile equilibrium maintained. The result is all too visible. Modern India is a vast landscape of raucous disharmony, and more than ancient sages to explain the nature of eternal unity, today India requires wise men to explain our current disharmonies, observers to explain our continued denial of what is living in favor of what is shining—and in the process perhaps to provide a bridge between our past and our present.

I suppose the scholar G. V. Desani could be called a modern wise man. He certainly has the credentials. He spent fourteen years as an ascetic, traveling India, studying philosophy, and performing rigorous physical disciplines to understand the connection between India's ancient knowledge and her present confusions. When he found himself stranded in England during World War II, out of sheer homesickness he wrote his glorious novel, *All About H. Hatterr.*

Mr. Hatterr is a bankrupt Eurasian living in Bombay whose friend Mr. Banerji finally gets him a job on an Indian newspaper writing about various sages—the guru of Bombay, the guru of Madras, and so on. Each of the seven gurus Hatterr encounters, grown rich from the credulity of followers, gives him a philosophical lesson on Living. Hatterr's attempts to apply these lessons to his own life lead to a great Adventure, taking him inadvertently toward an enlightenment that he describes to his friend Mr. Banerji:

"As to *Truth*, the great generalisation is, *Dam mysterious!*"

Through the eyes of his amateur reporter, part-Asian, part-Western, in the center of contemporary Indian chaos, Desani uses the most complicated schools of Indian philosophy to exhibit the Indian comedy—that play of illusions at the center of her metaphysics. It is a brilliant feat of intellect, and to achieve it he has invented an Indian English of such energy that reviews of *All About H. Hatterr* by T. S. Eliot and Edmund Wilson and E. M. Forster expressed amazement and the British writer Angus Wilson described Desani's prose as "a Whole Language . . . like the English of Shakespeare."

But the story continues—through the author. Returning to India with his reviews, Desani, like his hero, tries to find employment writing for the magazine *The Illustrated Weekly*. The editor refuses to believe he is admired by such distinguished literary figures as T. S. Eliot and suggests Desani has written the reviews himself. Upset that his veracity is in dispute, Desani retires into a concrete chamber and enters a yogic trance, lowering his metabolic rate until he is in

a state of suspended death. Thus he remains until the editor makes an abject apology.

But then, as Hatterr notes on the first page of
his book:

WARNING!
Improbable, you say?
No, fellers.
All improbables are probable in India.

It is an incident worthy of the pen of the cartoonist Laxman, who records India for the national newspaper, the *Times of India.*

If India needs a contemporary account of the
great play of Maya, it need only look at
Laxman's daily report on power to the nation.
And the politics of India have provided Laxman
with a contemporary mythology as packed with
overwhelming personalities, as elaborate, as full
of color and incident as the power struggles described in the *Mahabharata.* But our egalitarian
times lack an epic grandeur, so it is only fitting
that they should be recorded by Laxman's bemused common man, who, with the startled
look of someone who has chanced upon a theat-
rical performance, occupies the corner of every
Laxman cartoon. Observing the increasingly bizarre behavior of India's public figures from this
vantage point, he watches the machinations of

megalomania to which its perpetrators are oblivious, his dazed expression puncturing the elaborate self-delusions of the human race better than the maxims of a sage.

The common man of Laxman's cartoons peoples the novels written by his brother, R. K. Narayan.

The titles of Narayan's novels—*The Bachelor of Arts*, *Mr. Sampath The Printer of Malgudi*, *The Financial Expert*, *The English Teacher*, *The Vendor of Sweets*—suggest their modest world enclosed in the fictitious small town of Malgudi, which is itself half village and half contemporary urban India, allowing Narayan to observe the collision between the two while creating a range of characters whose lives have chronicled the life of modern India.

In *The Guide* a petty criminal escapes from jail and seeks sanctuary in a temple, pretending to be a holy man. When a drought occurs, the villagers believe that only his holy powers can end it, and so they help him to fast until the rains come—Indian mendacity confronting Indian superstition in a struggle of life and death.

In *The Painter of Signs* a simple man who prides himself on his calligraphy is hired to paint population-awareness signs by a militant feminist from the city with whom he falls in love. His courtship of her provides an elegant display of the encounter between traditional and modern India. In *The World of Nagaraj* a man who wishes only to write a great thesis on the paradoxes of the sage Narada finds he cannot think because his nephew has married a girl who plays screeching Indian film music all day long in the hopes of becoming a playback singer in the movies. But which is the greater crime— vulgarity or withdrawal from the world to pursue the arcane?

It is our good fortune that two such gifted brothers should have happened to live in India during our first half-century of freedom, as if the gods knew we desperately required our own great satirist and our own great ironist to keep us sane. Their combined work could stand alone and still provide a record of India's first fifty years as an independent nation.

And the energy with which the philosopher, the cartoonist, the novelist have confronted modern India should dispel Tagore's fears of the country's continued withdrawal from "the fraud of creation." The great thing is, their work also gives us a choice, withdrawal or participation. Now we have guides for both.

So I find my own suffering better alleviated by laughing every morning at Laxman's wry view of India than by contemplating my navel. But yoga makes my laughter last longer.

When Graham Greene says Narayan's works have offered him a second home, it has also made Indians more comfortable in theirs. If those homes are built by the methods of the Vastushastra, so much the better, but when the reality beyond the walls seems too jarring to be endured, Narayan's irony makes it tolerable.

And when mandalas and mantras and the Ayurveda's herbal tonics all fail to cure the panic attacks induced by India's mounting chaos, we can always turn for solace to Hatterr's hard-won enlightenment.

Then his creator, G. V. Desani, yogi and thinker and teller of tales, instructs us to plunge recklessly back into the sea of India, cheering us on with the philosophical injunction:

"Carry on, boys, and continue like hell."

34

The Shape of Things

In 1912, shortly before he received the Nobel Prize for Literature, Rabindranath Tagore was asked to write a poem honoring George V on his coronation as King Emperor of India. The irritated poet composed instead a hymn in praise of the God who was:

Supreme leader of the minds of all people,
Ruler of India's destiny.
Punjab, Sind, Gujarat, Maharashtra,
  Dravida, Orissa, Bengal,
The Vindhyas, Himalayas, Jumna and
  Ganga,
The waves of her swelling oceans
Waken, taking your name,

Asking your blessing,
Singing your glory.

The hymn became the national anthem of a
free India, and years ago, when my son was only
five years old, he told me another story about
gods and India. I have since tried to find out
where he might have learned the story, because
he doesn't remember and no one else seems to
know it. I have consulted Sanskrit scholars in
Varanasi and looked through books on Indian
legends, but I haven't succeeded in finding its
origins. Maybe the story is his own, a child's
explanation of the birth of his country. Or the
interpretation he gave to his grandparents' de-
termination to give him a country.

In any case, the background to the story is
this. Shiva is deep in meditation in an ice-locked
cave in the Himalayas. The goddess who loves
him has been banished from his sight, lest she
disturb his meditation. She wanders the world,
trying to forget the great ascetic, determined not
even to turn and look in his direction. But she
cannot help herself, and standing on a wave in
the Indian Ocean, she turns and stretches her
arms toward the mountains, beseeching the ascetic god to enter her embrace. Into the space
between her arms explode rice fields and deserts
and rivers and stone fortresses and elephants

and glaciers and coconut palms and temples—in short, the continent of India.

"That is why," my son informed me, stretching his arms toward me in a semaphore of embrace, "India is this shape."

Perhaps it needs a child to recognize there is a force pulling into itself every tragic disparity, every dispersion of race and language and religion, every confusion that is India, inspiring in its peoples a feeling larger than patriotism, what they stretch out their arms to reach. Tagore called it a geography made sacred by devotion. I can't say what it is, only that when I am away it pulls at me, and I long for the land shaped by longing.

35

Leisure Activity

The word *firdauz* in Urdu means divine leisure. It is used to acknowledge the gift of something so unique only God could have crafted it when he had nothing else on his mind. And so we say, God made it at his leisure. The expression is sometimes used to describe:

The smell of the Indian evening—smoke from burning leaves mixing with the smoke of burning cow dung and the incense of evening devotions
The scent of parched earth during the monsoon rains when peacocks fan their tails to dance
The green sweep of parakeets crossing the sunset

Kites wheeling in a becalmed sky

Pyramids of gaslights preceding a bride-groom seated on a white horse, and wedding bands playing "A Summer Place" in march time

Drying saris spread across a river sandbank

The soothing shadow of rice fields at dusk

The harsh light of the desert and mica glittering in the sand

The sound of cowbells over car horns, the gentle eyes of Indian cows meandering through city streets until they sit down in the center of the road in clumps and you know it is going to rain

The noise of crows at daybreak, dew glistening on cobwebs

The clanging of bells in an Indian temple, crying babies held on the hips of veiled women

The bell sounding from the neck of an elephant plodding down a city avenue

The ankle bells of the dancer

Film music blaring from tea stalls, the hypnotic litany of the street vendor

The solitary flute of the mountain goatherd haunting the empty hills

The steady drone of chanting monks around the tree where the Buddha reached enlightenment

The cry of the muezzin, *There is no God but God*, and the ecstatic singing of the quawaalis

The warning cough of the tiger, the cobra hissing in a basket

The popping of water lilies, the snarling of pi-dogs, the koyal bird crying for rain

Idols floating into the ocean, garlands disintegrating in the tide

The white horizon of the holy Himalayas

The shriek of the train whistle, coal dust on wooden seats, a river crossing at nighttime

Jasmine and marigold garlands wet from a bucket of water

Glass bangles sold by lantern light, fragile color fracturing the dark

The rustle of starched muslin against the limbs, the warmth of stone floors under bare feet

The cooling of henna on the palm, the smoothness of brown skin under the hand

Spices stacked in triangles—orange turmeric, red chilies, gray cumin, black mustard seeds

The scents of Indian perfumes—attars of vetiver and sandalwood, of jasmine and opium; a drop of attar of roses made from a thousand petals of the thousand-petaled rose; and the attar called leisure

The smear of color on a Hindu woman's forehead, the silver ornaments plaited into a Muslim girl's hair, the angular earrings in a tribal woman's earlobes, the bright turban on a northern Indian's head, the austere shawl on a southern Indian's shoulders, the muslin mask across a Jain monk's mouth, the saffron robe of the celibate, the matted locks of the ascetic

Bread swelling like a cloud on the platter, white rice steaming on the banana leaf, a yard of coffee cooling between steel glasses

A clay pot beading the hand with moisture, a bamboo spoon grazing the tongue

The village tank, the marble dome, the step well

An assembly of men pulling at hookahs between the taproots of a banyan tree

Lanterns swaying from a bullock cart, the blaring horns of painted lorries

The stench of an Indian bazaar—flowers, incense, overflowing gutters, dust, petrol, sticky sweets

The assault on the senses
The caress of the senses
Surely God made India at his leisure.

POLITICAL CHRONOLOGY

1947

- August 14/15, British Empire transfers power to the new nations of India and Pakistan. East and West Pakistan separated by land mass of India.
- British Empire announces details of Partition awards.
- August–September, seven million people cross borders; religious killings leave over a million dead.

1947–1948

- Integration of independent kingdoms into India and Pakistan. Ruler of Kashmir joins India following invasion by tribesmen from Pakistan.

Pakistan retains invaded territory. United Nations oversees Kashmir cease-fire line.

1948
- Mahatma Gandhi assassinated by Hindu fanatic.

1950
- Constitution of India adopted.
- Chinese troops enter Tibet.

1951
- First Indian general election. Jawaharlal Nehru returned as Prime Minister, leads Indian National Congress to victory in three general elections.
- First Five Year Plan of economic development inaugurated.

1959
- State government of Kerala dismissed.
- China annexes Tibet as Dalai Lama takes sanctuary in India.

1962
- India-China War on Tibetan frontier.
- Chinese troops enter India through state of Assam.

1964

- Death of Nehru. Shastri new Prime Minister of India.
- Green revolution in agriculture launched.

1965

- India-Pakistan War on two western fronts, Kutch and Kashmir.

1966

- Shashtri dies in Tashkent during Indo-Pakistani peace conference convened in Soviet Union.
- Nehru's daughter, Indira Gandhi—no relation to Mahatma Gandhi—appointed interim Prime Minister of India by National Congress.

1969

- National Congress splits into factions.

1971

- In fifth general election, Indira Gandhi wins landslide victory with slogan "Remove Poverty"; changes party name to Congress (Indira).
- Revolt in East Pakistan; crackdown by Pakistani Army.
- Nearly ten million East Pakistani refugees cross into Indian states of Assam and Bengal.
- India-Pakistan War.
- East Pakistan becomes nation of Bangladesh.

1975
- Justice Sinha of the Allahabad High Court finds Indira Gandhi guilty of electoral malpractice.
- State of Emergency imposed on India.

1977
- General election—Janata Party wins; Morarji Desai becomes Prime Minister.

1979
- General election called.
- Bhindranwale campaigns with Indira Gandhi's candidates.

1980
- Seventh general election; Indira Gandhi becomes Prime Minister.
- Sanjay Gandhi crashes aircraft over capital and is killed.
- Bhindranwale and his followers take up residence in Golden Temple of Amritsar, Punjab.

1981
- Rajiv Gandhi elected Member of Parliament.

1982
- India commences arming of Sri Lankan Tamils.

1984

- State government of Kashmir replaced.
- Indian Army sent into Golden Temple.
- General election called.
- Indira Gandhi assassinated by Sikh guard; Rajiv Gandhi becomes acting Prime Minister.
- Sikhs attacked in Delhi. Government claims 2,300 Sikhs killed in two days; Citizens' Committee places figure at over 4,000.
- Rajiv Gandhi wins general election and becomes Prime Minister.

1985

- Supreme Court rules all wives are entitled to civil alimony for the maintenance of themselves and their children.

1986

- Rajiv Gandhi government passes new law making Indian Muslim women subject to medieval interpretations of Islamic shariat law.

1987

- India invades Sri Lankan airspace to drop supplies to Sri Lankan Tamils.
- India–Sri Lanka peace talks.
- Indian Army invited to Sri Lanka to disarm Tamil insurgents.

1988

- Disputed mosque at Ayodhya opened.
- Agitation begins for construction of Hindu temple at disputed site.

1989

- Foundation stone laid at Ayodhya for construction of Hindu temple.
- Ninth general election won by National Front coalition; V. P. Singh becomes Prime Minister.
- Indian Army brought back from Sri Lanka after 1,500 Indian soldiers killed fighting Tamil separatists.

1990

- V. P. Singh enforces job and educational quotas for lower castes; riots follow.
- Hindu nationalist party—Bharatiya Janata Party—launches nationwide agitation for building of Ayodha temple.
- Government puts security cordon around disputed site, jails agitators.

1991

- General election called.
- Rajiv Gandhi blown up by Tamil woman guerrilla wired as a human bomb.
- Narasimha Rao becomes Prime Minister of minority Congress (Indira) government.

- Reform of Indian economy, tax structure.
- State elections in Punjab.

1992
- Mosque at Ayodhya demolished; Hindu-Muslim riots follow.

1993
- Ten bombs explode across Bombay; hundreds killed or injured.

1996
- General election. BJP wins largest number of seats but not enough to form government.
- Deve Gowda of Janata Dal Party becomes Prime Minister, heading thirteen-party coalition.
- Those accused in 1984 Sikh killings sentenced, including ministers from Rajiv Gandhi government; compensation paid to victims' families.
- State elections in Kashmir.
- Senior political leaders and government officials face trial on corruption charges; many sentenced to jail.

1997
- I. K. Gujral of Janata Dal Party becomes Prime Minister of coalition government.
- K. R. Narayanan, belonging to India's most oppressed caste, becomes head of state as President of India.
- India celebrates fifty years as a democracy.

ACKNOWLEDGMENTS

Seven essays in this book have appeared in different form in the following places: Channel Four Television, U.K.; *House and Gardens* magazine, U.S.; *Sunday Times* of London, U.K.; *New Delhi* magazine, India; *The Pleasure of Reading* (Bloomsbury Publishing, U.K.); *Resurgence* magazine, U.K.; *FMR* magazine, Italy.